Cambridge Elements ☰

Elements in Organization Theory
edited by
Nelson Phillips
Imperial College London
Royston Greenwood
University of Alberta

T0316687

CULTURAL ENTREPRENEURSHIP

A New Agenda for the Study of Entrepreneurial Processes and Possibilities

Michael Lounsbury
University of Alberta

Mary Ann Glynn
Boston College

CAMBRIDGE
UNIVERSITY PRESS

CAMBRIDGE
UNIVERSITY PRESS

University Printing House, Cambridge CB2 8BS, United Kingdom

One Liberty Plaza, 20th Floor, New York, NY 10006, USA

477 Williamstown Road, Port Melbourne, VIC 3207, Australia

314–321, 3rd Floor, Plot 3, Splendor Forum, Jasola District Centre,
New Delhi – 110025, India

79 Anson Road, #06–04/06, Singapore 079906

Cambridge University Press is part of the University of Cambridge.

It furthers the University's mission by disseminating knowledge in the pursuit of education, learning, and research at the highest international levels of excellence.

www.cambridge.org
Information on this title: www.cambridge.org/9781108439275
DOI: 10.1017/9781108539487

© Michael Lounsbury and Mary Ann Glynn 2019

This publication is in copyright. Subject to statutory exception and to the provisions of relevant collective licensing agreements, no reproduction of any part may take place without the written permission of Cambridge University Press.

First published 2019

A catalogue record for this publication is available from the British Library.

ISBN 978-1-108-43927-5 Paperback
ISSN 2397-947X (online)
ISSN 2514-3859 (print)

Cambridge University Press has no responsibility for the persistence or accuracy of URLs for external or third-party internet websites referred to in this publication and does not guarantee that any content on such websites is, or will remain, accurate or appropriate.

Cultural Entrepreneurship

A New Agenda for the Study of Entrepreneurial Processes and Possibilities

Elements in Organization Theory

DOI: 10.1017/9781108539487
First published online: January 2019

Michael Lounsbury
University of Alberta

Mary Ann Glynn
Boston College

Abstract: This Element provides an overview of cultural entrepreneurship scholarship and seeks to lay the foundation for a broader and more integrative research agenda at the interface of organization theory and entrepreneurship. Its scholarly agenda includes a range of phenomena from the legitimation of new ventures, to the construction of novel or alternative organizational or collective identities, and, at even more macro levels, to the emergence of new entrepreneurial possibilities and market categories. Michael Lounsbury and Mary Ann Glynn develop novel theoretical arguments and discuss the implications for mainstream entrepreneurship research, focusing on the study of entrepreneurial processes and possibilities.

Keywords: cultural entrepreneurship, entrepreneurship, organization theory, culture

© Michael Lounsbury and Mary Ann Glynn 2019

ISBNs: 9781108439275 (PB), 9781108539487 (OC)
ISSNs: 2397-947X (online), 2514-3859 (print)

Contents

1 A Cultural Approach to Entrepreneurship

Over the last few decades, research on cultural entrepreneurship has grown dramatically, providing one of the most exciting opportunities at the interface of organization theory and entrepreneurship scholarship (e.g., Gehman & Soublière, 2017; Lounsbury, Cornelissen, Granqvist, & Grodal, forthcoming; Lounsbury, Gehman, & Glynn, forthcoming; Lounsbury & Glynn, 2001). The notion of *cultural entrepreneurship* was initially seeded by DiMaggio's (1982, 1986) influential research on high culture or "highbrow" organizations, such as art museums, opera houses, symphony halls, and theatres, in nineteenth-century Boston. DiMaggio showed how these upper-crust institutions emerged as distinctive organizational forms as a result of efforts by urban elites to distance themselves from the masses (and their popular entertainment), as a means to cement their own standing in society. His findings succeeded in documenting the organizational basis for wide-scale cultural change and ignited a broader conversation about the organizational production of culture in processes of entrepreneurship, situating it at the intersection of cultural, economic, and organizational sociology. Over time, research in this tradition has expanded to focus not only on elite art institutions and products, but also on mass-produced and mass-consumed cultural products, such as popular music, books, and artwork, produced in modern societies (e.g., DiMaggio, 1986; Griswold, 1994; Hirsch, 1972, 2000; Peterson, 1977). Although DiMaggio's seminal work was tethered to the establishment of new organizational and institutional forms, our work presumes a looser coupling between these forms and cultural entrepreneurship; in doing so, we seek to extend this line of scholarship in several important ways in this Element.

To start, we build upon and extend our prior efforts (e.g., Glynn & Lounsbury, 2005; Lounsbury, Gehman, & Glynn, forthcoming; Lounsbury & Glynn, 2001, 2005; Wry, Lounsbury, & Glynn, 2011) to generalize beyond DiMaggio's notion of cultural entrepreneurship at the institutional level to understand how *all forms of entrepreneurial action are fundamentally constituted by similar kinds of cultural processes.* Our initial proposition (Lounsbury & Glynn, 2001) asserted that *at the core of all entrepreneurial initiatives is a process of meaning-making (e.g., the telling of stories) that aims to construct an optimally or legitimately distinctive organizational identity in a focal institutional field.* To the extent that these communicative efforts are successful, and resonate with key audiences, an entrepreneurial initiative is more likely to gain legitimacy and access to needed or desirable resources. In our framework, culture is a critical element in entrepreneurship, for both the entrepreneurs, who use it as a resource in the symbolic construction of their enterprises, and for the audiences, who evaluate and legitimate these enterprises and potentially endow entrepreneurs with necessary assets.

For instance, Martha Stewart cultivated an entrepreneurial identity via story-telling that resonated profoundly with millions of consumers in the 1990s, enabling Stewart's rise to prominence as a brand (Glynn, forthcoming). A key component underlying Stewart's rise to prominence was her first television show, "Martha Stewart Living," a one-hour program in which she dispensed information, displayed expert techniques, demonstrated a variety of home-keeping techniques, and ladled advice on a variety of domestic activities ranging from cooking and gardening to ironing, pet-keeping, flower arranging, collecting, and decorating for Christmas. Ironically, the television syndicator that finally took a chance on the show initially questioned the content that Stewart intended to deliver and challenged her ability to read the culture, to "get" what television audiences wanted:

> Who was going to eat thirty minutes of How to Cut Your Roses in Detroit? This was a suicide mission. The next segment was something about how to make compost heaps . . . "I'm not sure I can sell this . . . I mean maybe we can sell it, but I'm not sure we'll get renewals. . . . Martha, I mean, look, the people in the cities where we have to sell this show are in urban environ-ments. They're working class people. These people don't even have gardens." Martha looked back at him. Her voice was even and cool, conveying the total confidence in her words as she said, "yes, but they want them." [Byron, 2002: 212]

The stories Martha told on her show did resonate widely. "Martha Stewart Living" aired for thirteen years, from 1991 to 2004, attracting a large and loyal audience in Detroit and other urban markets throughout the United States, eventually winning 13 Daytime Emmy Awards, and receiving 47 Emmy nominations. Over that time, she "had become ubiquitous, the face of the age" (Byron, 2002: 195). Her eponymous show was cancelled at the beginning of 2004, following Martha Stewart's conviction on four felony charges. Martha's cultural narrative endured, however, in spite of her trial and tribula-tions; as Barbara Walters described it: "Her [Stewart's] rise and fall were of Shakespearean proportions" (20/20 Interview, 11/24/2003). Martha's entrepre-neurship highlights the critical role of culture in entrepreneurship, illustrating how story-telling is vital to entrepreneurial identity construction and to culti-vating resonance with key audiences that enable resource acquisition and wealth creation – the main aspects of our original framework.

Since our original theoretical statement nearly two decades ago (Lounsbury & Glynn, 2001), the literature on cultural entrepreneurship has broadened to include a diverse range of studies on entrepreneurs, organizations, and wider socio-economic change involving a wide variety of cultural resources and processes (e.g., Granqvist, Grodal, & Woolley, 2013; Johnson, 2007; Kennedy, 2005; Ravasi & Rindova, 2008; Rindova, Petkova, & Kotha, 2007; Santos & Eisenhardt, 2009; Uberbacher, 2014; Weber, Heinze, & Desoucey, 2008). Along with the growing attention to culture in organization and management theory (Weber & Dacin, 2011), and related fields (Friedland & Mohr, 2004), the cultural entrepreneurship literature has also been inflected by a proliferation of cultural conceptualizations as diverse as institutional logics, institutional work, frames, vocabularies, categories, rhetoric, stories, narratives, discourse, communication, and so on (Giorgi et al., 2015; Lounsbury et al., forthcoming; Thornton, Ocasio, & Lounsbury, 2012; Vaara, Sonenshein, & Boje, 2016). While we are excited by these developments, we worry that the emergence of so many ways of talking about and studying culture risks fragmentation of scholarship, inhibiting knowledge accumulation and progress. One of our hopes with this Element is to contribute to the development of a more synthetic conversation about cultural processes in the study of organizations, entrepreneurship, and markets. To do so, we provide an overview of cultural entrepreneurship scholarship and seek to lay the foundation for a broader and more integrative research agenda. Building on, and expanding, our initial definition (Lounsbury & Glynn, 2001), we conceptualize cultural entrepreneurship as the *processes by which actors draw upon cultural resources (e.g., discourse, language, categories, logics, and other symbolic elements) to advance entrepreneurship or to facilitate organizational or institutional innovation.* This includes a range of phenomena from the legitimation of new ventures, to the construction of novel or alternative organizational or collective identities, and, at even more macro levels, to the emergence of new entrepreneurial possibilities and market categories. In the following section, we provide a broad overview of key aspects of the literature on cultural entrepreneurship.

1.1 The Current State of Entrepreneurial Studies

Interest in entrepreneurship has grown exponentially in recent decades, becoming a focal point for public policy makers around the globe who have embraced it as a panacea for problems related to innovation, growth, and development (Aldrich, 2012). Entrepreneurship is also a burgeoning field of academic inquiry, albeit still a young one. It was only a little over three decades ago when the top specialty academic journal in the area, the *Journal of Business Venturing*, as well as the Entrepreneurship Division of the Academy of Management, which fosters research on "the emergence of entrepreneurial opportunities and/or new economic activities" (aom.org/Content.aspx? id=237#ent), were established.[1]

Before this time, entrepreneurship was a relatively marginalized topic of study for variegated disciplinary researchers in psychology, sociology, and economics. Although it would be unfair to characterize entrepreneurship research as fledgling, it continues to be an applied area of focus that has little indigenous theory to give it a disciplinary character. Although there are now a large number of researchers trained in business schools who self-identify as entrepreneurship scholars, and who have worked hard to construct boundaries around the domain of entrepreneurial research, the complex and wide-ranging nature of entrepreneurial activities has invited a more transdisciplinary approach to the topic (Aldrich & Ruef, 2006; Gartner, Bird, & Starr, 1992).

Nonetheless, the discipline of economics has had a dominant imprint on the field of entrepreneurship (Foss, Klein, & Bjørnskov, forthcoming); this is perhaps unsurprising given the high status of economics as a discipline (Fourcade, 2009). And yet, this is somewhat ironic given that neoclassical economics had characterized entrepreneurs as virtually invisible since no variable exists to represent the exercise of entrepreneurship in econometric models designed to explain sources of productivity variation (Baumol, 1983). In this vein, Arrow (1983: 15) described the entrepreneur as a "lightning calculator, the individual who rapidly scans the field of alternative productive processes and chooses the optimum at any given set of prices." This efficient market conceptualization reminds one of "the old joke about the assistant professor who, when walking with a full professor, reaches down for the $100 bill he sees on the sidewalk. But he is held back by his senior colleague, who points out that if the $100 bill were real, it would have been picked up already" (Olson, 1993: 3).

To be fair, most economic-oriented scholars interested in entrepreneurship have avoided the canon of mainstream economics, instead embracing Austrian economics, especially the work of Schumpeter (1934), who envisioned the entrepreneur as a bold-thinking, charismatic leader who could generate disequilibria by combining resources in novel ways, catalyzing a process of "creative destruction" (see Swedberg, 1991). In contrast to neoclassical economics, the Austrian school of economics provides a richer conceptualization of entrepreneurs emphasizing arbitrage – where entrepreneurs discover

---

[1] The *Journal of Business Venturing* was created in 1985, and the Entrepreneurship Division of the Academy of Management was established in 1987. Note that before formal divisions are created at the Academy of Management, groups of researchers interested in coalescing form interest groups. An entrepreneurship interest group initially formed in 1971.

and exploit slight disequilibrium opportunities, thereby ensuring that markets remain as close as possible to an equilibrium state (Kirzner, 1973). Kirzner's work has provided an important foundation for contemporary management research on entrepreneurship, which, anchoring on Shane and Venkataraman's (2000: 218) now classic agenda-setting statement, focuses on the "study of sources of opportunities; the processes of discovery, evaluation, and exploitation of opportunities; and the set of individuals who discover, evaluate, and exploit them" (see also Korsgaard et al., 2016; Venkataraman, 1997). In essence, entrepreneurship is popularly conceptualized as the proverbial triumvirate: a jockey (the individual entrepreneur or founder), a horse (the new venture or idea), and the track (the broader market, economic, political, or social environment).

And yet, in spite of such advances, entrepreneurship scholarship has been plagued by three biases – the start-up bias, the opportunity-discovery bias, and the sole individual bias (Foss & Klein, 2012). The start-up bias tends to equate entrepreneurship solely with start-ups or new ventures (e.g., Gartner & Carter, 2003), neglecting how entrepreneurship occurs in a wider variety of organizational contexts, including established firms such as in corporate "intrapreneuring" (e.g., Helfat & Peteraf, 2009; Hitt et al., 2002; Ireland et al., 2003; Kazanjian, Drazin, & Glynn, 2002; Pinchot, 1985). Of course, the start-up bias also reflects the empirical fascination with fast-growing commercial enterprises and their venture capital funders, diminishing attention to social entrepreneurs and social innovation.

The opportunity-discovery bias refers to the overly narrow explanatory focus on the psychological or cognitive aspects of opportunity discovery (e.g., Baron, 1998; Shane, 2003), leaving black-boxed the more dynamic processes that link entrepreneurial perception to opportunity exploitation efforts that include the assembly of resources (Foss & Klein, 2012; Sarasvathy, 2008). In addition, trait-based psychological approaches to entrepreneurship have failed to uncover robust linkages among personality characteristics (e.g., need for achievement), entrepreneurship, and entrepreneurial performance (Aldrich & Wiedenmayer, 1993; Gasse, 1982). As we argue in this Element, the emergence of what we label "entrepreneurial possibilities" requires a more deeply contextualized social scientific approach.

The sole-individual bias has to do with the overwhelming focus in the literature on modeling entrepreneurs as heroic individuals, neglecting the extent to which entrepreneurship involves teams (Aldrich & Zimmer, 1986; Felin & Zenger, 2009; Ruef, 2010; Ruef, Aldrich, & Carter, 2003; Stewart, 1989) and wider collective action (Burress & Cook, 2009; Lounsbury, 1999; Lounsbury, Ventresca, & Hirsch, 2003; Sine & Lee, 2009; Wry, Lounsbury, & Glynn, 2011). The emergence of entrepreneurial possibilities that enable new kinds of ventures and initiatives is often best understood from the perspective of interaction and collective action in the context of institutional fields (Padgett & Powell, 2012; Schneiberg & Lounsbury, 2017; Seidel & Greve, 2017), necessitating perhaps a multilevel approach or one that addresses entrepreneurship at higher levels of analysis.

These three biases – start-up, opportunity-discovery, and sole-individual – have hampered opportunities for broader dialogue between entrepreneurship and other scholars in organization and management theory, sociology, anthropology, and cognate areas who seek to contextualize entrepreneurship in wider communities and institutional fields (e.g., Aldrich & Ruef, 2006; Jennings et al., 2015; Thornton, 1999). We seek to enable this integration and, in particular, argue that the framework of cultural entrepreneurship affords a fruitful entry point for a richer interdisciplinary or multilevel approach to entrepreneurship.

We believe that this is timely because much of contemporary entrepreneurship research exhibits an impoverished approach to understanding the cultural dynamics that consequentially shape core aspects of the entrepreneurial process (Lounsbury & Glynn, 2001). This is perhaps not so surprising, given the dominance of economic approaches in entrepreneurship research. For instance, in Foss and Klein's (2012) ambitiously laudable effort to develop an entrepreneurial theory of the firm that extends Knight's (1921) work on judgment under conditions of uncertainty, i.e., the judgment-based approach, culture is given limited attention. In fact, theory related to cultural processes, central to much of the organization and management theory literature (Giorgi et al., 2015; Weber & Dacin, 2011), is not substantively engaged in a wide variety of prominent pieces in the entrepreneurship literature, including those by Shane and Venkataraman (2000) and Alvarez and Barney (2007). Here, we seek to redirect the attention on culture in the process of entrepreneurship.

1.2 Cultural Entrepreneurship

Despite the shortcomings of the current entrepreneurship literature, it is important to note that culture has not been absent from broader conceptualizations of entrepreneurs and entrepreneurial processes. Going back to Max Weber's influential tome, *The Protestant Ethic and the Spirit of Capitalism* (1992 [1904]), there have been many attempts to identify cultural groupings, such as those based on religion, race, ethnicity, or geography, that could explain the sources of entrepreneurial activity (Ruef & Lounsbury, 2007). In the 1960s, the development of a social deviance or ethnic marginality perspective posited that cultural groupings of entrepreneurs emerge at the periphery of dominant value systems (e.g., Hoselitz, 1963). The Examples of such entrepreneurial groups include the Antioqueños in Colombia, Bataks in Indonesia, Ilocanos in the Philippines, and refugee groups such as the Cubans and Indochinese in the United States (Shapero & Sokol, 1982). This prefigured the development of a cottage industry of research on ethnic and immigrant entrepreneurship emphasizing the subcultural dimension of ethnicity (e.g., Aldrich & Waldinger, 1990; Light & Rosenstein, 1995; Portes, 1995; Zhou, 2004).

Relatedly, researchers have shown the importance of geographic clusters, communities, networks, and ecosystems in organizational behavior (e.g., Marquis, Lounsbury, & Greenwood, 2011). Noting that a geographic locale "can be bounded in terms of neighborhoods and cyberspace ... [and that] their boundaries may not be material- and resource-based, but instead cognitive- and culture-based" (Thornton & Flynn, 2003: 405), the notion of "place" as an influential environment figures importantly in cultural entrepreneurship. Perhaps the most prominent example of this is Silicon Valley (Kenney, 2000), where the web of spatial and relational networks creates opportunities for innovation and for garnering needed resources. In recent years, there has also been a growing literature on female entrepreneurship (e.g., Hughes & Jennings, 2015; Jennings & Brush, 2013). Although early work in this area echoed the literature on ethnic and immigrant entrepreneurship, treating culture as a discriminated social category (Etzkowitz, Kemelgor, & Uzzi, 2000), scholarship of late has begun to engage the feminist studies literature and adopt a cultural lens to explore the gendered nature of entrepreneurial processes writ large (Ahl, 2006; Cliff, Langton, & Aldrich, 2005). This domain of entrepreneurial scholarship offers a more substantive engagement with contemporary theories of culture and cultural studies.

Somewhat relatedly, there has been some research on how societal-level cultural norms, role expectations, and social sanctions can impede or facilitate innovation and entrepreneurial activity (Gerschenkron, 1962; Martinelli, 1994). For instance, both Cochran (1949) and Lipset (1967) explained differences in the economic development of the United States and Latin America in terms of the degree to which entrepreneurship was legitimated. This view of culture as a generalized value system linked to economic institutions underlies much cross-country comparative research, including studies that have leveraged Global Entrepreneurship Monitor (GEM) data (www.gemconsortium.org). However, this work embraces a relatively thin conceptualization of culture emphasizing its structural features (Hofstede, 1980), resonating with old institutional approaches that imagine culture as a basket of homogenous norms and generalized value systems, at societal or subgroup levels, that become internalized into one's personality via socialization (Parsons, 1937). This process of value infusion, rooted in Freudian ego-psychology, is theorized to provide a core foundation (and function) for the maintenance of social order.

This approach to culture has been widely critiqued over the past several decades (e.g., DiMaggio & Powell, 1991; Granovetter, 1985; see Giorgi, Lockwood, & Glynn, 2015, for a review). In the 1960s, the functionalism of Parsons was rejected in the context of unrest animated by socio-cultural conflict connected to race, class, gender, ideology, and other dimensions of societal difference that were masked by then-dominant strands of social theory. In this milieu, a wide variety of perspectives emerged. In sociology, conflict theory, Marxism, and the study of social movements became ascendant (Stark, 2007). Symbolic interactionist and ethnomethodological research programs also emerged, conceptualizing society as a complex, ever-changing mosaic of subjective meanings (e.g., Berger & Luckmann, 1967; Garkinkel, 1967; Goffman, 1967).

With respect to the conceptualization and study of culture, one of the biggest shifts came in the form of the *cognitive revolution* that redirected attention away from widely shared norms and values and towards taken-for-granted routines and beliefs (DiMaggio, 1997; DiMaggio & Powell, 1991). This was seeded by Berger and Luckmann's (1967) treatise on the social construction of reality and subsequent developments such as Bourdieu's theory of practice and notion of habitus (1977). This unfolded alongside a more general cultural turn across the social sciences (e.g., Giorgi, Lockwood, & Glynn, 2015) that, in contradistinction to the dominance of rational actor approaches, emphasized the role of symbolic meaning systems in shaping the behavior of actors (Friedland & Mohr, 2004).

Some approaches to culture, including those theorized by organizational institutionalists (DiMaggio & Powell, 1983; Scott, 2014), have been critiqued for their emphasis on isomorphic conformity that some compared to the imagery of socio-cultural stasis and shared values that permeated Parsonsonian sociology (e.g., Hirsch, 1997). However, this line of scholarship, along with the general cognitive turn in cultural research (DiMaggio, 1997), both radically altered and energetically catalyzed a flowering of research on cultural processes in organization and management theory (Weber & Dacin, 2011). In contradistinction to approaches to culture that emphasized fairly stable ideational systems that constrained thought and action, some began to ask about the multiplexity of culture (e.g., Kraatz & Block, 2008; Martin, 1992; Phillips & Hardy, 1997; Smircich, 1983; Swidler,

1986; Weick, 1995). In addition, instead of concentrating on how culture provides a structural constraint, researchers began to emphasize the enabling and constitutive aspects of culture (Dobbin, 1994; Meyer, Boli, & Thomas, 1983) and that culture could function as a resource for actors, to be used as a kind of toolkit of possibilities to construct strategies of action in different kinds of contexts (Swidler, 1986).

These shifts underlie new theoretical programs of research such as the institutional logics perspective (Thornton, Ocasio, & Lounsbury, 2012) that focuses on how cultural pluralism enables multiple forms of rationality and the ability for actors to more actively and strategically manipulate cultural elements in their efforts to construct, maintain, and renegotiate local and trans-local practice orders. The rise of practice theories and process approaches that embrace flatter ontologies has reinforced these developments (Glaser, forthcoming; Lounsbury & Crumley, 2007; Schatzki, 2003; Schatzki, Knorr-Cetina, & Savigny, 2001; Smets, Aristidou, & Whittington, 2017). These new approaches give primacy to the role of culture and provide new opportunities to understand varied aspects of social and economic life, including the sources and consequences of entrepreneurial behavior. To date, entrepreneurship scholarship has had limited engagement with these developments.

The concept of "culture" elides a consensual definition in the management literature and is studied with varied ontologies and epistemologies across disciplines. However, Spillman (2002: 4) usefully argues that "the central concerns of those who study culture are to understand processes of meaning-making, to account for different meanings, and to examine their effects in social life." The now-voluminous literature on cultural entrepreneurship is one expression of this.

Since cultural entrepreneurship has become a widely invoked label (Gehman & Soublière, 2017), it is important to distinguish what we are up to in relation to empirical studies of entrepreneurship in the so-called "creative" or "cultural" fields such as art, architecture, fashion, music, film, and the like. In the context of those fields, cultural entrepreneurship is conventionally conceptualized as an innovative activity that generates cultural value and/or wealth via the creation of novel cultural products, services, or forms (Askin & Mauskapf, 2017; Jones, Sapsed, & Lorenzen, 2015; Khaire, 2017; Leadbeater & Oakley, 1999). In addition to the many studies of entrepreneurship in the arts and other creative fields (e.g., Kolb, 2015; Sorin & Sessions, 2015), this understanding of cultural entrepreneurship is reinforced and promoted by a variety of programmatic efforts such as *The Deans' Cultural Entrepreneurship Challenge* organized by Harvard University's i-lab. It is a start-up competition that provides resources and support to the best new venture idea that "unites artistic and entrepreneurial visions to create and maintain ventures with the financial, social, and organizational infrastructure necessary for arts and artists to survive and thrive" (https://i-lab.harvard.edu/deans-challenge/cultural-entrepreneurship).

In this spirit, many universities now offer courses, workshops, and even degree programs in cultural entrepreneurship to encourage and support the creation of such new ventures; for example, see the University of British Columbia's workshop (https://cstudies.ubc.ca/courses/online-workshop-cultural-entrepreneurship/uc011) and related specialties like music entrepreneurship (e.g., music.cmu.edu/pages/music-entrepreneurship). Along with this growing interest in new ventures in cultural fields, there have been significant efforts, supported by the Kauffman Foundation and others, to facilitate the design of city, regional, and national-level policies that enhance such new venture creation and sustainability (Markusen, 2013). In this milieu, entrepreneurial support organizations such as the Creative Startups Accelerator, founded in 2007 in Santa Fe, New Mexico, have emerged to foster geographically situated creative communities.

While entrepreneurship in the arts and other creative fields is a substantively important activity, there have been sustained efforts to develop cultural entrepreneurship as a scholarly idea that accounts for a wider variety of socioeconomic processes and outcomes, including entrepreneurial efforts in high technology, in large, traditional bureaucracies, and in efforts aimed at generating social change. Favoring the development of more generalized claims and theory, our aim in advancing cultural entrepreneurship scholarship is not to focus on what is unique and special about the arts and creative fields, but to understand the commonality of entrepreneurial processes across very different kinds of contexts. Following Geertz (1973: 5), we believe that culture is everywhere as we are all "suspended in webs of significance" that we spin. Accordingly, one of our core claims is that understanding the pervasiveness of culture and focalizing cultural meaning-making provide novel insights about general mechanisms and processes that shape the sources and consequences of entrepreneurship across space and time.

Thus, over the past couple of decades, we have sought to develop a more expansive, dynamic, and multilevel approach to cultural entrepreneurship (e.g., Glynn & Lounsbury, 2005; Lounsbury & Boxenbaum, 2013; Lounsbury & Glynn, 2001; Navis & Glynn, 2010, 2011; Wry, Lounsbury, & Glynn, 2011; Zhao, Ishihara, & Lounsbury, 2013). Theoretically, we have drawn on, and contributed to, nascent efforts to link scholarship on organizational institutionalism (Greenwood et al., 2017; Scott, 2014) and identity (Elsbach & Glynn, 1996; Elsbach & Kramer, 1996; Gioia, Schultz, & Corley, 2000; Glynn, 2000,

2008, 2017; Glynn & Abzug, 2002; Grimes, 2018; Whetten, 2000; Whetten & Godfrey, 1998). In doing so, our approach to cultural entrepreneurship, which we elaborate on in this Element, draws attention to the importance of micro-processes and the cross-level mechanisms that link actors and their identities to wider organizational and institutional dynamics. Our argument embraces both the "toolkit" approach, which looks to culture as providing critical resources that actors manage to develop strategies of action (Swidler, 1986), as well as how culture constitutes actors, institutional fields, and entrepreneurial possibilities.

1.3 The Organization of the Element

The Element is organized as follows. In section 2, we provide an overview of cultural entrepreneurship research and our initial 2001 framework. In revisiting our original theorization, we highlight our conceptualization of story-telling as both a dependent variable (an outcome of entrepreneurial identity formation) as well as an independent variable (as a touchstone for resonance that enables legitimacy and resource acquisition). We situate our discussion in relevant literatures, particularly works focusing on developments at the interface of institutional and identity scholarship in organization studies. This helps to uncover the range and depth in how the idea of cultural entrepreneurship has been developed, highlighting areas requiring further research including the expanded range of symbolic management tools and practices that comprise cultural entrepreneurship.

In section 3, we draw on recent developments in the study of culture in organization and management theory and related fields to map out a broader theoretical and empirical research agenda that focuses on the contextual dynamics of cultural entrepreneurship. As part of this effort, we highlight how a focus on the sources and consequences of optimal distinctiveness could be fruitful. In section 4, we develop the implications of our arguments for mainstream conversations in entrepreneurship, focusing on how a cultural entrepreneurship approach can breathe new life into the study of entrepreneurial opportunities by redirecting research to the study of entrepreneurial possibilities in institutional fields. Finally, in section 5, we conclude the Element with a summary of our core arguments and advance a new agenda for the study of entrepreneurial processes and possibilities.

2 The Cultural Entrepreneurship Framework

In this section, we provide a review of the initial cultural entrepreneurship framework as articulated by Lounsbury and Glynn (2001), highlighting those aspects that have been more or less developed in the subsequent scholarship, as well as the expansions suggested by this body of scholarship. As indicated in the previous section, cultural entrepreneurship research is rich and diverse. Topically, it has been wide ranging, going beyond the study of for-profit entrepreneurs (e.g., Martens, Jennings, & Jennings, 2007), to address corporations (e.g., Rindova, Pollock, & Hayward, 2006), nonprofits and community foundations (e.g., Graddy & Wang, 2009), social innovation (e.g., Nicholls, 2010; Slade Shantz, Kistruck, & Zietsma, 2018), institutional fields (e.g., Hardy & Maguire, 2010), incubators (Tracey, Dalpiaz, & Phillips, 2018), crowdfunding platforms (e.g., Gegenhuber & Naderer, forthcoming), work role transitions (e.g., Ibarra & Barbulescu, 2010), mega-projects (e.g., Srinivasan & Johri, 2013), drug courts (e.g., McPherson & Sauder, 2013), and religious organizations (e.g., Giorgi, Guider, & Bartunek, 2014).

Theoretically, this body of work has been informed by new developments in the conceptualization and study of culture – including those in the institutions and identity literatures, as well as in cultural sociology (e.g., Swidler, 1986) that advance a more agentic understanding of culture as a "toolkit" of elements that could be creatively and strategically accessed and deployed by actors in different situations (e.g., Lingo & O'Mahony, 2010). Empirically, the literature has expanded beyond the individual level of analysis of storytelling on which the original theorization focused (Lounsbury & Glynn, 2001) to embrace an understanding of distributed, collective storytelling (e.g., Navis & Glynn, 2010; Wry, Lounsbury, & Glynn, 2011).

The core aspects of our initial arguments are depicted in Figure 1. We defined cultural entrepreneurship as "the process of storytelling that mediates between extant stocks of entrepreneurial resources and subsequent capital acquisition and wealth creation" (Lounsbury & Glynn, 2001: 545). In our framework, we position the entrepreneurial narrative as a central mechanism of the entrepreneurial process, although it functions in two discrete ways: as both a dependent variable – the outcome of the entrepreneur's theorization of, and identification with, stocks of capital – and an independent variable, as a driver of new venture legitimation and resource acquisition (see appropriate arrows in Figure 1). With this model, we sought to highlight the role of entrepreneurs as "skilled cultural operatives" (p. 559), i.e., as active agents capable of tapping cultural resources to construct firm identity and attain legitimacy in an institutional field.

In our theorization, the entrepreneur was imagined as a sort of cultural bricoleur, forging a sensible and compelling narrative from cultural elements borrowed from arenas that were both unique to the nascent venture

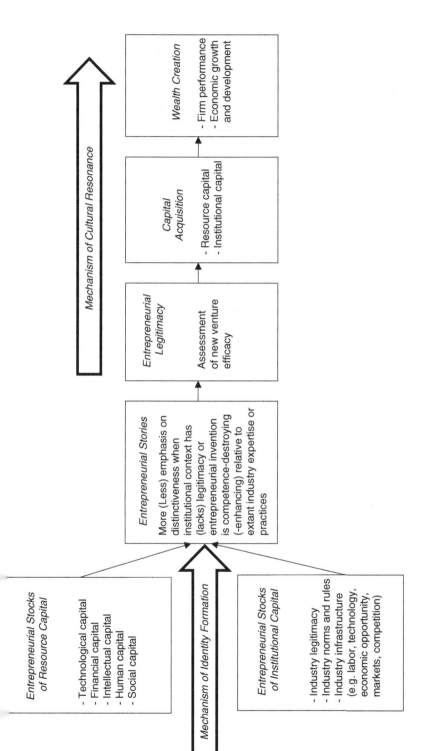

Figure 1 A Process Model of Cultural Entrepreneurship
(Adapted from Lounsbury & Glynn, 2001)

("Extant Stocks of Resource Capital") and institutionally sanctioned in the broader societal, regional, or industry environment ("Extant Stocks of Institutional Capital"). Thus, entrepreneurship was explicitly embedded in its resource environment with the critical act of entrepreneurship being the choice of the appropriate cultural elements from the institutional toolbox. With these tools in hand, the entrepreneur had to weave them into a coherent narrative that would both rationalize the purpose and functioning of the new venture – establishing its identity – and make it comprehensible, meaningful, and appealing to relevant audiences. If the narrative struck the right chord, it would serve to legitimate the new venture and enable the flow of vital human, institutional, technological, financial, economic, or other resources that could help fuel and grow the new firm. Thus our arguments focused on two general kinds of mechanisms – identity formation, evident in the entrepreneurial narrative, and cultural resonance or alignment with key audiences who might bestow it with both intangible and tangible resources.

At a meta-theoretical level, our focus on how actors can be skilled cultural operatives who culturally can shape how different kinds of audiences understand, evaluate, and reward them became a core idea in the development of cultural entrepreneurship scholarship (Fisher, Kotha, & Lahiri, 2016). While we conceptualized entrepreneurial action as embedded in a broader cultural milieu at the intersection of institutions and identity, the wider research agenda we aimed to set became backgrounded in the subsequent literature that focused more on story-telling en route to the legitimation of new entrepreneurial ventures (Überbacher, 2014). Nonetheless, this focus on stories and the narrative construction of identity (e.g., Barry & Elmes, 1997; see more recently, Vaara, Somenshein, & Boje, 2017; Grimes, 2018) has been important and illuminating, and has become a growing way in which culture has infiltrated our understanding of entrepreneurship and related areas such as leadership.

Like the "effective leaders" that Bennis (1996: 160) described, effective entrepreneurs "put words to the formless longings and deeply felt needs of others. They create communities out of words. They tell stories that capture minds and win hearts." Stories can thus become powerful means of communication and persuasion, imparting meaning to ambiguous events, and catalyzing action (Brown, Gabriel, & Gherardi, 2009; Gabriel, 2000; Weick & Browning, 1986; Zilber, 2007). The importance of stories has become ever more crucial in contemporary society as evidenced in the growing importance and impact of TED talks (see Gallo, 2016). In the context of entrepreneurial start-ups, Navis and Glynn (2011) demonstrated empirically that such identity narratives about "who we are" and "what we do" provide institutional primes that guide investor sensemaking and decisions to invest in new ventures (see also Gartner, 2007; Garud, Gehman, & Giuliani, 2014; Garud, Schildt, & Lant, 2014; Hjorth & Steyaert, 2004; Mantere et al., 2013). Storytelling is also crucial in the context of entrepreneurial pivoting (McDonald & Eisenhardt, forthcoming; McDonald & Gao, 2017).

Martens, Jennings, and Jennings (2007) empirically demonstrated the power of identity narratives. They analyzed the structure and content of entrepreneurial stories for all semiconductor, biotechnology, and Internet content provider firms that filed their intent to issue an IPO on the NYSE, NASDAQ, or AMEX stock exchanges between mid-1996 and the fall of 2000. Their study showed that effectively constructed stories enable entrepreneurs to acquire resources that enable growth and development. Emphasizing the need to better understand the role of the media in identity construction, Rindova, Pollock, and Hayward (2006) argue that dramatic narratives constructed at the interface between firms' nonconforming behavior and storytelling, and the media construction of celebrity identity narratives (see also Hayward et al., 2004; Sine et al., 2007), enhance the economic opportunities of firms. Their argument extends cultural entrepreneurship arguments beyond the realm of start-ups to include larger and more mature organizations. Moreover, their focus on dramatic narratives also makes clear that stories told do not necessary need to reflect any objective reality to be effective; for some, identity narratives may provide some sort of façade (Abrahamson & Baumard, 2008), while for many others, such stories are a key component of reality construction (Boje, 1991; Bruner, 1991).

Although stories are a powerful mechanism by which identity is constructed (Czarniawska, 1997), they are but one tool in an entrepreneurial organization's cultural toolbox (Swidler, 1986). Scholars have highlighted a broader array of symbolic management skills (Ashforth & Humphrey, 1997; Feldman & March, 1981; Pfeffer, 1981; Weick, 1995; Westphal & Park, forthcoming) that enable effective construction and communication of the entrepreneurial identity. For instance, based on an intensive field study of U.K. entrepreneurs, Zott and Huy (2007) showed that the skillful use of symbolism, such as in presentations to investors, better enabled resource acquisition. In particular, they highlighted the importance of symbolically imbued communications that emphasized the entrepreneur's personal credibility, their ability to professionally organize, organizational achievement, and the quality of their stakeholder relationships. Cornelissen and Clarke (2010) argue that communications that involve inductive, analogical, or metaphorical reasoning provide a platform for the creation and commercialization of novel ventures, enabling legitimacy and resource acquisition (see also Cornelissen, Holt, & Zundel, 2011).

In their study of the emergence and evolution of U.S. satellite radio, Navis and Glynn (2010) showed that the legitimation of this new market category went hand-in-hand with shifts in intra-category firm attention; over time, this changed from the legitimation of the category as a whole to the differentiation of the firms' individual identities. Their findings empirically validate a core proposition of Lounsbury and Glynn (2001). Going beyond the analysis of identity narratives, Navis and Glynn also highlight the importance of other symbolic devices, i.e., linguistic frames and press announcements of reputable affiliations and endorsements, legitimating both the firms themselves and the broader institutional milieu (e.g., market category) in which they are embedded. To date, we have amassed a good deal of research on the breadth of cultural resources utilized in efforts to gain legitimation and favorable audience attention, including names (Glynn & Abzug, 2002; Zhao, Masakazu, & Lounsbury, 2013), labels (Granqvist, Grodal, & Woolley, 2013), prototypes and concepts (Seidel & O'Mahony, 2014), product design (Dalpiaz, Rindova, & Ravasi, 2016), and other symbols and forms of communication (Ravasi & Rindova, 2008; Rindova, Petkova, & Kotha, 2007).

Thus, research on cultural entrepreneurship subsequent to the 2001 publication of Lounsbury and Glynn's conceptual framework has illuminated several of the facets and processes that they originally theorized. Lounsbury, Gehman, and Glynn (forthcoming) summarize these accumulated findings and show how they have elaborated the 2001 framework. They note how the emergent literature has pushed towards a more processual understanding of entrepreneurial storytelling, including how stories are revised, draw on varied cultural resources, and have relational, temporal, and performative dimensions (Garud, Gehman, & Giuliani, 2014). They highlight how research has further elaborated on how processes related to entrepreneurial identity and legitimacy are shaped by institutional contexts, multiple audiences, and the interrelation of sensemaking and sensegiving. They also note how the initial focus on wealth creation has begun to expand to more generally account for value creation in non-economic spheres, and how scholars have begun to more explicitly emphasize the iterative and recursive relationships between identity, legitimacy, and storytelling on the one hand, and value creation and storytelling on the other hand. They offer an "expanded" theory of cultural entrepreneurship (see Figure 2) that incorporates these insights including a richer conceptualization of entrepreneurship as embedded in, and constitutive of, cultural context.

However, many lines of development in this expanded view remain tentative and relatively unexplored. While we believe that many pathways for future

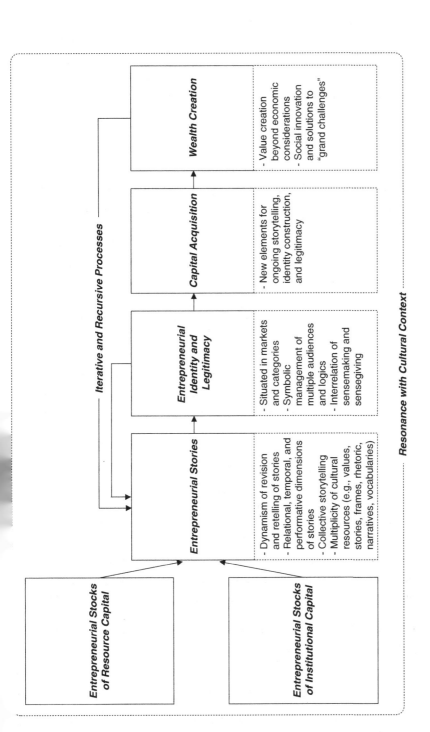

Figure 2 Expanded Theoretical Model of Cultural Entrepreneurship
Adapted from Lounsbury, Gehman, & Glynn (forthcoming)

research will be fruitful and await interested researchers, here we focus on elaborating a future-oriented agenda that focuses on core questions related to identity and institutions. In particular, we believe that more attention needs to be paid to how actors construct, access, and employ cultural resources in order to cultivate identity and gain legitimacy, how these processes are institutionally conditioned, and how they generate effects. For this, we believe that cultural entrepreneurship scholarship needs to more deeply contextualize the actors and processes analyzed.

To start, we propose that the cultural entrepreneurship research agenda must continue to expand beyond the legitimation of new commercially oriented ventures. As Foss and Klein (2012: 222) argue, all behavior is, in a broad sense, entrepreneurial, and should therefore not be treated as a separate domain of social scientific analysis. We could not agree more. To wit, the promise for "cultural entrepreneurship" research is the cultivation of a more general cultural approach to the bridging of micro and macro realms of entrepreneurial action in and around institutional fields. As a step in this direction, below we aim to more fully flesh out our initial cultural entrepreneurship framework, focusing on the key mechanisms underlying the sources and consequences of storytelling.

Returning to the original Cultural Entrepreneurship framework (Figure 1), it is useful to think of identity narratives as both a *dependent variable*, i.e., the entrepreneurial identity constructed and expressed as a narrative outcome, in the first stage of the process, and then, as an *independent variable,* i.e., an antecedent to the acquisition of legitimacy, firm capital, and wealth, in the second stage of the process. The initial phase of cultural entrepreneurship is one of identity construction, whereby the entrepreneur appropriates the "right" cultural tools from both his/her unique stocks and available institutional capital to craft in story form the "legitimate distinctiveness" of the new venture (Navis & Glynn, 2011). The second phase is one whereby this cultural narrative functions to help legitimate the venture and acquire needed resources; to do this, the narrative needs to resonate with the new venture's key stakeholders. We elaborate on each these phases, as well as the general mechanisms under-lying the processes, in an effort to lay the groundwork for a wider research agenda on cultural entrepreneurship, which we develop further in the next two subsections.

2.1 Phase I: Identity Formation

The opening move in the process of cultural entrepreneurship, we argued, is one of crafting a compelling identity story. The elements of this story are appropriate from the entrepreneur's available cultural repertoire, which consists of capital sourced from both his/her idiosyncratic resources and the institutional resources from the culture milieu within which an enterprise is embedded. The cultural entrepreneur both "picks" the right cultural tools from each of these resource wellsprings and fashions them together to craft a coherent, compelling, innovative story. This initial step is one of identity formation, which becomes the bedrock of the entrepreneurial narrative; it involves facets of both institutionalism and identity.

The literatures on institutions and identity are two of the more prominent conversations in organization and management theory that have embraced the cultural turn and provide general theory for the study of entrepreneurial processes such as identity formation (Glynn, 2008; 2017; Lounsbury & Glynn, 2001; Thornton, Ocasio, & Lounsbury, 2012; Weber & Dacin, 2011). Here, we provide brief overviews of these two literatures that are intertwined in cultural entrepreneurship. We then discuss how we might draw on these two literatures to motivate and inform research on identity formation in cultural entrepreneurship.

Organizational Insitutitonalism. Although there does not exist a single general theory of institutions, the label "institutional theory" is colloquially used to refer to theoretical conversations in sociology, economics, political science, and organization studies that emphasize the role of durable traditions and arrangements in shaping various kinds of behavior (Scott, 2014). This transdisciplinary literature is vast, employing disparate ontological approaches and definitions of institutions. For instance, much of institutional economics conceptualizes institutions as formal rules that provide constraints, and relies on reductionist, rational choice assumptions to explain the behavior of actors given the institutional constraints faced. The sociological and organizational literatures tend to rely a bit more on ontological skepticism, the rejection of rational choice approaches that instrumentalize behavior, and conceptualize institutions more as socio-cultural constructions that both constrain and enable different kinds of behaviors. One of the key differences across these two general paradigmatic approaches to institutional theory is that rational choice economic approaches tend to ignore the processes by which the decision making of actors is variously shaped and informed by cultural processes and meanings, essentially conceptualizing people and organizations as acultural information processors that are able to achieve optimal outcomes by evaluating costs and benefits. Sociological and organizational approaches tend to be more critical about the ontological nature of the actor, and focus on how the identity of people and organizations, as well as their very ability to act, is culturally constituted and shaped. They go further to argue that what is "rational" is culturally contingent and varies across time and space.

Our emphasis here is on the organizational institutionalism literature, which is informed by sociological and management scholarship (Greenwood et al., 2017), thus offering a very different theoretical starting point relative to most economistic approaches to entrepreneurship and institutions. Organizational institutionalism emanated from sociology and research in organization and management theory in the 1970s, and continues to be a dominant and dynamic theoretical tradition (Lounsbury & Beckman, 2015). DiMaggio and Powell (1991) argued that the "new institutionalism" of the 1970s and 1980s developed as a cultural approach to the effects of organizational environments on organizational decision making and practice. This theoretical domain contrasted with, and explicitly developed in reaction to rational choice theory and instrumental approaches to behavior. As Schneiberg and Clemens (2006) argue, institutional theory is an anti-reductionist approach that seeks to explain the behavior of organizations and other actors as resulting from higher-order contextual effects rooted in wider institutional systems such as fields and world society. A major focus in the early development of institutional theory was on legitimacy as the key driver affecting organizational resource acquisition, survival, and performance.

Research has documented how organizations gain legitimacy by conforming to (or becoming isomorphic with) institutionalized practice models (or rationalized myths) which become key aspects of cultural environments within which organizations are embedded, rather than by acting in accord with technical efficiency (Meyer and Rowan, 1977; Meyer & Scott, 1983; Meyer, Boli, & Thomas, 1986). DiMaggio and Powell (1983) prominently argued that highly structured fields generate a profound legitimacy imperative resulting in isomorphic pressures that lead to organizational homogeneity via coercive, mimetic, and normative forces. Studies of organizational legitimacy constitute a broad literature in their own right (e.g., Deephouse & Suchman, 2008; Johnson, 2004; Stryker, 1994; Suchman, 1995). Suchman (1995) highlighted three different forms of legitimacy invoked in the literature: pragmatic legitimacy rooted in the self-interest of evaluators; moral legitimacy grounded in the normative approval of key audiences; and cognitive legitimacy, which rests on the understandability and taken-for-grantedness of the kind of object or actor being evaluated.

Empirical research in institutional theory in the 1980s and into the 1990s focused a great deal on uncovering various mechanisms related to isomorphism and organizational legitimacy (for overviews, see Strang & Soule 1998 and

Boxenbaum & Jonsson 2008). However, by the end of the 1980s, critiques began to emerge about the dominant theoretical and empirical emphasis on isomorphism, which downplayed microprocesses and organizational variation in favor of what some saw as a theory of structural determinism (DiMaggio, 1988; Greenwood & Hinings, 1996; Hirsch, 1997; Hirsch & Lounsbury, 1997). This first led to a new emphasis on institutional entrepreneurship and change that tended to feature narratives of heroic actors who were able to overcome structural barriers (for reviews, see Hardy and Maguire, 2008; Battilana et al., 2009). This gave way to more nuanced cultural approaches to agency that emphasized its more distributed nature (Garud et al., 2014; Jones et al., 2011; Lawrence & Suddaby, 2006; Lounsbury & Crumley, 2007) as well as the multiplicity of cultural meanings that vary across space and time (Ferraro, Etzion, & Gehman, 2015; Thornton, Ocasio, & Lounsbury, 2012; Weber, 2005). Although early research in this tradition counterposed technical efficiency demands to institutional pressures in order to document the pervasiveness of isomorphism (e.g., Tolbert and Zucker 1983), subsequent research has argued that technical demands are institutionally constructed and has aimed to show how isomorphism itself can be quite variegated and uneven across space and time (e.g., Ansari et al. 2010; Lounsbury, 2007).

Organizational Identity. While research on organizational identity (see, e.g., Pratt et al., 2016, for a review) initially began as a separate theoretical conversation from institutional theory, its similar embrace of the primacy of culture and the centrality of meaning has enabled fruitful bridging between these perspectives over the past two decades. As Glynn (2008) has argued, there are two main streams of organizational identity scholarship – one that is more organization-centric, which derives from the domain of psychology, and one that is more focused on the relationality between organizations and alters in their institutional environment, which derives from the domain of sociology. The former is anchored on how organizational identities are unique and individuated, because they are constituted by central, distinctive, and enduring organizational attributes (Albert & Whetten, 1985). The latter concentrates on how organizational identities are interrelated, and situated, in institutional spaces, and how broader collective identities provide shared cognitive and normative orientations for the construction of organizational identity (e.g., Cornelissen, Haslam, and Balmer 2007; Ocasio, Mauskapf, & Steele, 2016; Pratt 2003; Wry, Lounsbury, and Glynn 2011).

Relational approaches to organizational identity provide a natural bridge to institutional theory since they emphasize how organizations are positioned relative to each other in a broader institutional field that is comprised of multiple identity positions. Although an emphasis on isomorphism leaves little room to explore questions of organizational identity since all organizations end up looking alike, the shift towards a focus on organizational heterogeneity linked to fragmented socio-cultural environments (Thornton, Ocasio, & Lounsbury, 2012) has created new opportunities to explore issues of identity construction. Pedersen and Dobbin (2006) argue that institutional environments provide a cultural grammar of identity markers from which organizations can choose, enabling organizations to appear broadly similar to each other, while also allowing the cultivation of organizational distinctiveness via the translation and tailoring of symbolic elements.

This fundamentally altered research on legitimacy, which initially had been invoked as part of the conceptual apparatus underpinning explanations of isomorphism and organizational conformity to audience expectations. New questions began to be asked about how organizations acquire and manage legitimacy, with the reconceptualization of organizations as strategic actors that had to become skilled cultural operatives (Aldrich & Fiol, 1994; Lounsbury & Glynn, 2001; Rao, 1994). Legitimacy itself became conceptualized in more multidimensional ways, where institutional environments were understood as more fragmented and offering varied sources of legitimacy for organizations (Ruef & Scott, 1998). Contemporary research in this vein has shown how institutional fields may be fragmented into multiple kinds of organizational forms that generate distinctive collective identities in relation to each other in varied domains such as healthcare (Ruef, 2000), mutual funds (Lounsbury, 2007), and higher education (Kraatz & Zajac 1996).

Several scholars also began to examine the relationship between institutional change and organizational identity (Czarniawska & Wolff, 1998). For instance, Elsbach and Kramer (1996) showed how institutional pressures related to the emergence of business school rankings were perceived as a threat, leading to strategic responses by business schools to emphasize their distinctiveness in the face of powerful efforts to conceptualize them as objects to be compared and valued (see also Espeland & Stevens, 1998). Rao et al. (2003) documented how the creation of the French nouvelle cuisine logic facilitated a wider variety of chef and restaurant identities. There is also relevant work on the construction of organizational and collective identities such as organizational forms. Weber, Heinze, and Desoucey (2008) highlighted how a new grass-fed beef collective identity was constructed by mobilizing social codes across a distributed array of actors. Meyer and Hollerer (2010) showed how the identities of various actors in the field of Austrian corporate governance was shaped by how they framed issues of shareholder value in the context of competing neoliberal American and Continental European logics.

As Lounsbury and Glynn (2001) argue, even under conditions where isomorphic pressures exist, organizations will still aim to achieve some level of distinctiveness relative to peers (see also Deephouse, 1996, 1999; Durand & Calori, 2006; Zhao et al., 2017; Zuckerman, 2016). Drawing on Brewer (1991), they argue that firms aim to become "optimally distinct" as radical deviation from the dictates of collective identities may trigger a lack of understanding of what an organization is among key audiences who, as a result, may ignore such organizations (see Zuckerman, 1999). On the flip side, pure conformity may provide little strategic leverage to get noticed or competitive advantage that enhances performance outcomes (Barney, 1991). In developing their arguments, Lounsbury and Glynn (2001) focused on how organizational identity construction via story-telling is institutionally contingent. In particular, they argue that "the content of entrepreneurial stories will focus relatively less on establishing a venture's distinctiveness when the industry context within which the entrepreneur is embedded lacks legitimacy . . . [Conversely], the content of entrepreneurial stories will focus relatively more on establishing a venture's distinctiveness when the industry context within which the entrepreneur is embedded has been legitimated" (Lounsbury & Glynn, 2001: 559). In section 3, we extend our thinking about the formation of identity stories in Phase I by elaborating further on how a focus on optimal distinctiveness can help expand the scope of cultural entrepreneurship scholarship.

2.2 Phase II: Cultural Resonance of Identity Stories

In the process of cultural entrepreneurship depicted in Figure 1, the first stage, developing the distinctive entrepreneurial narrative, is followed by a second stage that maps the effectiveness of that narrative in appealing to resource providers who can endow the new venture with legitimacy, needed assets, and, ultimately, wealth in the context of commercial enterprises. If we apply the cultural entrepreneurship framework to other kinds of entrepreneurial initiatives – such as social enterprise – we may broaden the range of outcomes of interest to include enhancements to well-being and sustainability, as well as reductions in poverty, disease, and other maladies. Notwithstanding, the second phase of the framework takes up the question of cultural resonance, or how symbolic communications make sense and appeal to people; in other words, it concerns how cultural elements such as entrepreneurial narratives link in to those "aspects of a particular cultural schema [that] make it dominating, pervasive and enduring" (Swidler, 2001: 213). The mechanism through which this can be achieved is that of cultural resonance.

We theorize the entrepreneurial narrative as a framing device that packages and organizes information about the nascent venture, which brings "attention to a few stylized dimensions of reality, while hiding others" (Giorgi, 2017: 712), in order to explain and rationalize it to audiences. The effectiveness of such frames depends on their ability to "resonate," i.e., "match or align with the audience's beliefs, values, aspirations or ideas" (Giorgi, 2017: 712). The concept of resonance has been applied most often to the study of frames in social movements, but has more general utility in understanding processes of legitimation and audience receptivity (Cornelissen & Werner, 2014).

A frame is a kind of interpretive schema that simplifies and organizes the world, selectively filtering aspects of the environment, in order to enable actors to see, comprehend, and act in the world (e.g., Goffman, 1963; Snow & Benford, 1992). Frame alignment links the interpretive schema of an individual's values and beliefs to those of the organization or institution so that they appear congruent and compatible (Snow, Rochford, Worden, & Benford, 1986: 464). Framing efforts succeed when they are resonant or build on a "stock of folk ideas and beliefs" (Snow et al., 1986: 473–474). When frames are not resonant – or even contested – social movement activists typically initiate the process of "frame transformation" by reconstituting the meaning of what is going on and developing alternative frames that better align with conventional interpretive frames (Snow et al., 1986: 473–474). Thus, cultural resonance is dynamic, with alignment shifting as cultural sentiments or the cultural contexts shift over time. Moreover, resonance may not be dichotomous; rather, frames can be characterized by their "degree of resonance" (Snow et al., 1986: 477).

Framing achieves resonance through two main pathways: cognitive and emotional. Cognitive resonance, i.e., the alignment of a frame with an audience's beliefs or understandings, is predicated on familiarity, "the display of elements that are known or close to the intended audience ... because it establishes connections between a novel and an established domain" (Giorgi, 2017: 718). Emotional resonance "derives from a *felt* alignment of a frame with the audience's passions, desires or aspirations ... so that it moves or shakes a target recipient" (Giorgi, 2017: 721). Moreover, emotional resonance has a cultural undertone in that it "evoke[s] emotions that are in line with a predominant institutional ethos ... or an organization's culture" (Giorgi, 2017: 724). And, although they are conceptually distinct, cognitive and emotional resonance are pragmatically intertwined; both of these bases, together or separately, can be effective touchstones for achieving resonance through the framing of the entrepreneurial identity expressed through the narrative.

Identities are shaped by their cultural or institutional contexts (for a review see Glynn, 2008), but are also constructed by entrepreneurs who appropriate, assemble, and interpret cultural symbols, myths, or rituals that reference legitimate culture elements (Lamont & Lareau, 1988; Swidler, 1986) and link them to their venture (Ueberbacher, Jacobs, & Cornelissen, 2015). But such processes of identity bricolage are not random assortments of cultural symbols forged through cultural tools. Effective identities bundle cultural referents into "interpretive packages" that define core meanings of an organization (Gamson & Modigliani, 1989: 5). However, not all cultural symbols are equally potent for identity construction. Potent symbols "resonate with cultural narrations . . . the stories, myths and folk tales that are part and parcel of one's cultural heritage" (Snow & Benford, 1988); as a result, they appear natural and familiar and thus appeal because they invoke larger cultural themes already legitimated and taken for granted (Gamson & Modigliani, 1989: 5). Culturally potent identities leverage such symbols so as to have "narrative fidelity" (Snow & Benford, 1988) and demonstrate "cultural competence" (Bourdieu, 2007). As Dalpiaz and Cavotta (forthcoming) argue, the use of tainted cultural resources such as mafia symbols may be well recognized, but also entails resonance-related risk with some audiences. Thus, cultural resonance makes entrepreneurial identities encoded in stories appealing because of their association with meaningful symbols and broader cultural themes that are widely acceptable.

Cultural resonance can be articulated through any number of diverse cultural forms, styles, symbols, or content (Kubal, 1998) and actors can choose among the repertoires available in cultural toolkits (Swidler, 1986). Thus, although institutional alignment is a critical aspect of cultural resonance, it is not deterministic; actors' agency and interpretation of cultural proclivities affect the construction of identities and their capacity for cultural resonance. And, although cultural resonance would seem to have positive affects for new ventures and the process of cultural entrepreneurship (Lounsbury & Glynn, 2001), there has been little theoretical or empirical inquiry into this concept, in spite of work that hints at the significance of such an approach. The gap represents a fertile area for future research, one that becomes obvious when we consider the extant work on cultural entrepreneurship.

Although our initial cultural entrepreneurship framework (Lounsbury & Glynn, 2001) has been quite generative, enabling considerable knowledge accumulation on new venture legitimation processes, our understanding of identity formation and cultural resonance, and their interrelationships, remains underdeveloped. In addition, we need much more research on non-commercially oriented entrepreneurial ventures, as well as how different kinds of cultural resources are accessed and used in these processes. Such research would greatly assist in refining our understanding of the scope conditions on our initial claims and enable the development of more generalizable knowledge. Furthermore, we believe that there are great opportunities to expand the scope of cultural entrepreneurship scholarship. In this vein, the following sections sketch out some new directions for research on the contextual dynamics of cultural entrepreneurship and argue for a reorientation of research on "entrepreneurial opportunities" to focus on the construction and development of entrepreneurial possibilities in institutional fields.

3 Expanding the Scope: The Context of Cultural Entrepreneurship

As we have lamented earlier, although a sizeable literature on cultural entrepreneurship has developed over the past couple of decades, a great deal of it has focused on new venture legitimation (Überbacher, 2014), bracketing questions related to the institutional structuring of identities. This emphasis has zoomed in on entrepreneurs as "cultural operatives," which accords well with efforts in the wider literature to develop microfoundations (e.g., Powell & Colyvas, 2008; Thornton, Ocasio, & Lounsbury, 2012). However, although one may be interested in how new ventures are able to raise venture capital and grow, cultural entrepreneurship scholarship also suggests that an adequate understanding of such start-up success must go beyond the capabilities and human capital of a firm to understand how that firm positions itself in specific contexts to generate positive perceptions and to elicit favorable reactions by key stakeholders and other audiences.

That is, we posit that a more comprehensive understanding of cultural entrepreneurship would more deeply contextualize the behaviors of individual entrepreneurs within a wider institutional field. Although the literature has nicely attended to the microfoundations of entrepreneurship, particularly at the level of the individual founder or new venture, there has been a relative neglect of the macrofoundations of entrepreneurship. As suggested by Fine (1991), an adequate understanding of individual or organizational behavior also requires appropriate macrofoundations, or as cultural sociologists argue, a recognition of "the significance of the wider cultural repertoire from which social actors construct their strategies of action" (Spillman, 2002: 7). To move in this direction, we argue for the usefulness of a relational ontology (e.g., Bourdieu, 1984; Emirbayer & Johnson, 2008; Granovetter, 2017), which underpins institutional approaches to identity dynamics (Glynn, 2000) that were signaled but not fully developed in Lounsbury and Glynn (2001).

Relational approaches to social life have a long intellectual lineage, notably rooted in the work of Simmel (e.g., Simmel, 1990 [1907]; Simmel & Wolff, 1950) on social meaning and interaction, the work of Bourdieu (e.g., 1977, 1984), and in studies of culture and networks (e.g., DiMaggio, 1987; Emirbayer, 1997; Pachucki & Breiger, 2010). As Emirbayer (1997: 287) argues, "Relational theorists reject the notion that one can posit discrete, pregiven units such as the individual or society as ultimate starting points of sociological analysis (as in the self-actional perspective). Individual persons, whether strategic or norm following, are inseparable from the transactional contexts within which they are embedded." This imagery is core to organizational institutionalism, emphasizing how the identity of individuals and other collective actors can only be understood vis-à-vis how an individual is relationally situated, and involved in ongoing interactions, with other individuals in the context of an institutional field (Glynn, 2000).

The "field" concept has provided a central focal point for institutional analysis over the past four decades; many useful discussions and reviews exist (e.g., Martin, 2003; Wooten & Hoffman, 2008; Zietsma et al., 2017) that highlight several definitions used for the study of fields, noting that in organization theory most attention has been paid to fields organized around market exchange (DiMaggio & Powell, 1983) or issues (Hoffman, 1999); notably, fields can also be defined relative to cultural elements, including cognition or common meaning systems (Scott, 1995) or geography and spatial proximity (Marquis et al., 2011). And, although fields can be sites of conformity, via the forces of isomorphism, they can also be sites of conflict, contestation, and arenas of debate and change, particularly when they coalesce around issues.

Focusing on organizational fields, DiMaggio (1983: 149) prominently defined fields as including both the organizations that produce common outputs (whether these are automobiles, social services, or spiritual salvation) as well as the organizations that supply resources, effect constraints, or pose contingencies, particularly government agencies, trade associations, and professions (see also DiMaggio & Powell, 1983). Scott (2014: 106) provides a more general definition of field as "a collection of diverse, interdependent organizations that participate in a common meaning system." Given that fields can be identified and studied at various levels of analysis (Fligstein & McAdam, 2012), the more general notion of "institutional field" as opposed to "organizational field" has become more commonly used given that fields are institutionally defined and recognized spaces that contain a wide variety of actors and objects, importantly including but not limited to organizations of all varieties (Thornton, Ocasio, & Lounsbury, 2012).

Anchoring on the work of Bourdieu (e.g., 1977, 1984, 2000), we conceptualize institutional fields as relational spaces that can have multiple dimensions that clump or connect actors in different ways (Lounsbury & Ventresca, 2003; Zald & Lounsbury, 2014). These include concrete social network relationships, as well as cultural forms such as categories, classifications, conventions, and stories that provide meaning and help to differentiate actors and practices in a field. The structuring of a field also involves an understanding of authority relations, including the distribution of power and status (Delmestri & Greenwood, 2016; Jensen et al., 2011), as well as the role of authorized agents such as the state and professions that have legitimate authority to sanction or use violence to maintain order (Weber, 1978). The institutional field concept can be extremely useful for mapping how identities and identity positions, stabilized through entrenched power relationships, change as a result of strategic dynamics that involve ongoing re-negotiation of identities and identity positions (Fligstein & McAdam, 2012).

Given the cultural entrepreneurship focus on identities and institutions, Bourdieu's emphasis on socio-cultural relationality, and the processes whereby actors position themselves in a field, is particularly apropos. For instance, in describing fields of cultural production, Bourdieu (1983: 30) argues that

> the space of literary or artistic position-takings, i.e. the structured set of the manifestations of the social agents involved in the field – literary or artistic works, of course, but also political acts or pronouncements, manifestos or polemics, etc. – is inseparable from the space of literary or artistic positions defined by possession of a determinate quantity of specific capital (recognition) and, at the same time, by occupation of a determinate position in the structure of the distribution of this specific capital. The literary or artistic field is a field of forces, but it is also a field of struggles tending to transform or conserve this field of forces.

Although it goes well beyond the scope of this Element to fully engage Bourdieu's treatment of field, kinds of capital, commonality of beliefs (doxa), habitus, or other factors, there are a couple of key ideas from the aforementioned quote that we would like to highlight. Fields are institutional spaces where existing forces (emanating from what Bourdieu elsewhere calls "rules of the game") shape the identity positions of actors as well as the ongoing struggles actors engage in to create, maintain, or redefine their identities in order to achieve better outcomes – whether this involves access to resources, legitimacy, higher status, a better reputation, and the like. These ongoing struggles simultaneously involve a mixture of objective and subjective factors, canonically referred to as structure and agency (Golsorkhi et al., 2009). That is, the dynamic of fields in the work of Bourdieu must be understood as driven by the varied subjective identity projects and struggles of actors involved in a given field, as well as the more objective (or more durable and path-dependent) structures of socio-cultural relations among actors and practices that both enable and constrain the possibility space of identities (potential and realized), as well as the ongoing struggles related to identity creation, maintenance, or reformulation. As Friedland (2018:5) highlights, these processes are also infused with emotion:

> For Pierre Bourdieu all fields depend not just on their own principles of classification, but on an emotional investment, a "visceral commitment," an embodied "interest" in the stake within them (Bourdieu, 2000, pp. 98–99, 101–102). This is the energy of habitus, a "desire to be" (Bourdieu, 2000: 150) . . . Habitus, a manner of being "there" in the world, equips individuals with a capacity to enter, invest and act in a field, generating competition for the dominant form of capital thereby sustaining the illusio, "the unjustifiable investment," that what is at stake in a field actually has value (Bourdieu, 1984 , p. 250; Bourdieu, 1998; Bourdieu, 2000, p. 102; Friedland, 2009).

Bourdieu's work has animated a good deal of organization theoretic and sociological research, helping to provide an updated approach to culture that takes seriously social and political dynamics, while integrating agency and structure as a dialectical process. Thus, it is consistent with efforts to shift away from older, more deterministic notions of culture, and towards an emphasis on the multiplicity of culture, and the ability of actors (e.g., people and organizations) to creatively and strategically draw upon culture to navigate and enact their life-worlds (Milkie & Denny 2014; Swidler, 1986). That is, culture is no longer conceptualized as referring to the ultimate values underlying a nation-state or social group, but is studied with regard to the diversity of more localized meanings, practices, discourses, and repertoires (Lockwood et al., 2017; Mead, 1932; Pachucki & Breiger, 2010). From this perspective, people do not just live within a culture (or field) but actively access and use cultural elements as part of their sensemaking and sense-giving efforts. In line with what Bourdieu has argued, cultural sociologists today are generally in agreement that culture is simultaneously constraining and enabling (Alexander 2003; Hays 2000; Sewell, 1993). That is, culture consequentially affects social existence (people's behavior, choices, proclivities, etc.) and can be oppressive, but is also subject to change and transformation by social actors (Micelotta, Lounsbury, & Greenwood, 2017).

As emphasized in Lounsbury and Glynn (2001), stories and narratives are central cultural media by which actors cultivate their identities, understand, and make meaning in institutional fields. Fields provide a "cultural stock of stories" (Zilber, 2007: 1050) as well as "broadly available cultural accounts"

(Creed et al., 2002: 477). As Sartre (1938 [2000]: 61) famously wrote, "a man is always a teller of tales, he lives surrounded by his stories and the stories of others, he sees everything that happens to him through them; and he tries to live his life as if he were recounting it." Consistent with this claim, Harrison White (1992) argues that identity formation and stories provide key mechanisms that enhance our understanding of how actors navigate relational spaces such as fields. It is interesting to note that there is even a new domain of research emerging in economics, "narrative economics," that aims to understand how narratives become influential and spread (Shiller, 2017). While a focus on stories (or discourse more generally) does not allow for a comprehensive understanding of fields, we believe it can shed valuable light on core aspects of cultural entrepreneurship such as how organizations can become "optimally distinct" (Lounsbury & Glynn, 2001: 552) – especially in the context of extreme ambiguity that often encircles entrepreneurial action in emerging or dynamic institutional fields.

3.1 Optimal Distinctiveness: Cultural Entrepreneurship in and Around Institutional Fields

As noted in section 2, research on firm-level optimal distinctiveness is grounded in the question of how firms manage the tension between legitimacy pressures to appear similar to members or others linked to a category or institutional field, and those of audiences who value differentiation from the pack (e.g., Deephouse, 1999; Durand & Calori, 2006; Navis & Glynn, 2011). This tension is rooted in the historical divide between organization theory and strategy research. Although institutional theorists argued that firms aim to be similar to peers in order to gain legitimacy (e.g., DiMaggio and Powell, 1983), the field of strategy has alternatively focused on how firms gain competitive advantage by cultivating unique competencies rooted in valuable, rare, and inimitable resources (Barney, 1991; Helfat et al., 2007; Porter, 1996). Building on Brewer (1991), many have discussed that the resolution of this tension involves attaining "optimal distinctiveness" (Glynn & Abzug, 1998; Lounsbury & Glynn, 2001; Zhao et al., 2017; Zuckerman, 2017) – developing an identity in a field that resolves the tension between similarity and difference in a way that is appreciated by key stakeholders, and as a result, can help generate positive performance outcomes (Durand & Kremp, 2016; Garud, Schildt, & Lant, forthcoming; Philippe & Durand, 2011; Voronov, De Clercq, & Hinings, 2013).

Scholars initially proposed that optimal distinctiveness might be attained by strategically balancing the competing demands of conformity and differentiation, suggesting that a moderate level of novelty might be best (e.g., Deephouse, 1999). However, recent research on institutional fields has shifted attention away from a focus on isomorphism, and towards a more explicit focus on institutional multiplicity (e.g., the existence of multiple logics), making this initial solution to the bridging of institutional theory and strategy research anachronistic (Haans, forthcoming; Zhao et al., 2017). Our argument is not that the tension between similarity and difference is completely eliminated, but that it is more complex and multidimensional than originally conceptualized.

As research on categorization argues, to be evaluated by a field's key audiences, an organization first needs to be perceived to be a member of that field. Thus, while isomorphic pressures may not be so strong that organizations in a field are compelled to be identical, they must be perceived to be similar enough to other entities in a field in order to be evaluated as a member of a given field. Anchoring on the perceptions of third parties that evaluate organizations in a category, Zuckerman (2017) has argued for a two-stage valuation approach where once an organization is perceived as a legitimate member of a field, it may then be evaluated and valued relative to peers in a field.

From a research standpoint, this two-stage process suggests distinct kinds of questions. The first research question has to do with whether a firm is considered a member of a field, raising important issues about the boundaries of a given field and how key audiences including consumers, peer organizations, ratings agencies, media, and the like come to consider an organization a member of a field. To gain traction in this endeavor, it would be useful to have a more concrete definition and approach to the study of institutional fields. As Fligstein and McAdam (2012) argue, fields may exist at multiple levels from the world system, to industries, products, down to organizations and specific situations. They use the analogy of the stacking Russian dolls ("matryoshka") to say that fields are nested, leading to multi-dimensional cross-level effects and dynamics. Bourdieu argues that fields are an analytical construct of the researcher who is responsible for defining the object of analysis (i.e., an institutional field).

We take a slightly different approach, arguing that institutional fields are "real" insofar as they are widely recognized and treated as real social worlds (see Kennedy, 2005 for a similar approach to product market categories). Taking a decidedly cultural approach, *we define institutional fields as kinds of social worlds that are discursively segregated from other similar kinds of social worlds, and treated as relatively unique entities that are worthy of attention.* Without denying the importance of social and material elements, we believe that for fields to become objects of analysis and a perceptual focal point for action, they need to be linguistically demarcated as a thing to be discussed, regulated, invested in, and acted upon. For example, it is one thing for a local farmer to decide to cultivate crops without pesticides for a variety of reasons including its expense; it is an entirely different thing for large groups of farmers, consumers, food retailers, and government officials to gather together to build an organic food movement and industry – a field of action that emerged in opposition to the mainstream agribusiness field (Lee, Hiatt, & Lounsbury, 2017). Although field creation or emergence requires a great deal of cultural entrepreneurship, which itself is in need of further investigation (Padgett & Powell, 2012; Wry, Lounsbury, & Glynn, 2011), to analyze optimal distinctiveness in a given institutional field first requires that a given field be perceived to exist, and an understanding of how that field is situated amidst a community of fields.

That is, while institutional fields may exist as discrete discursive units, they must be understood as situated in relation to other fields whose boundaries may be more or less porous, and membership more or less fluid. Relatedly, some organizations may seek to define their identities in relation to similar organizations in a single field, while others may aim to define their identities across multiple fields (e.g., multinational corporations). So even though we may seek to analyze dimensions of similarity and difference in a single field, we must be aware of the contours of the field we seek to analyze. This includes developing an understanding of how producers as well as other key audiences (e.g., ratings agencies) perceive and talk about a field.

Analytically, this could be approached through an analysis of textual data and interviews where we can ascertain how various actors perceive a field. While some producers may tell stories that claim identities in a field, third parties may not recognize those producers as core members of a field. Even though Zuckerman (1999) provocatively showed that producers suffered penalties for not being perceived as core members of a field, we still have very little understanding of the mechanisms by which actors become recognized as core members of a field, and how this shifts over time. For this, we need to pursue more process-based analyses (Glaser, Fiss, & Kennedy, 2016; Glynn & Navis, 2013; Kennedy & Fiss, 2013). And although most of the research on optimal distinctiveness has focused on how firms position themselves in a single field, it may be that if we situate firms in a broader community ecology of fields, some firms achieve optimal distinctiveness and enhanced performance across several fields as opposed to within a single field. While this poses considerable challenges for cultural entrepreneurship scholarship, it also opens up new avenues for knowledge development.

However, it is fair to say that our understanding of optimal distinctiveness in single fields also remains relatively impoverished (Zhao et al., 2017). As we noted above, extant scholarship has focused too narrowly on the tension between isomorphic similarity and strategic difference, often analyzing organizational deviations from a mean on a single dimension of difference (e.g., commercial bank asset strategy in Deephouse, 1999). Embracing a more multidimensional conceptualization of fields, informed by a multiplicity of logics and identity positions (Greenwood et al., 2011; Kraatz & Block, 2008; Pahnke, Katila, & Eisenhardt, 2015; Reay & Hinings, 2009; Thornton et al., 2012), opens up new research possibilities. Research in this direction could be considerably advanced by embracing new methods inspired by the work of Bourdieu and the development of a "new structuralism" that draws on varied forms of network analysis and other techniques to measure and track multidimensional field dynamics in a way that is attentive to how behavior (e.g., entrepreneurial action) is embedded in and shaped by logics and broader forms of cultural classification (e.g., Breiger & Mohr, 2004; Höllerer, Daudigeos, & Jancsary, 2018; Lounsbury & Ventresca, 2003; Mohr, 1998; Mohr & White, 2008; Pachucki & Breiger, 2010).

These approaches were importantly incubated in a "measurement of meaning" working group in the Cultural Sociology section of the American Sociology Association in the early to mid-1990s (DiMaggio, 1994), as well as several "Cultural Turn" conferences organized at the University of California at Santa Barbara organized by John Mohr and Roger Friedland from 1997 to 2003 (Friedland & Mohr, 2004). Through all of these efforts, careful attention has been paid to how "meaning-centric approaches (in the more traditional, humanistic and interpretive sense of that term) mix with more formalized (measurement based) styles of looking and knowing and understanding cultural forms" (Mohr & Ghaziani, 2014: 229). It is important to emphasize that these different methodological styles, qualitative and quantitative, need not be conceptualized as antithetical – an unhelpful intellectual limitation promulgated by those whose identity has been constructed around the felt superiority of a particular method (Kaplan, 2015).

In their review, Pachucki and Breiger (2010) highlight several strands of contemporary research on culture and social networks that have emphasized how they are mutually constitutive. One important strand views "stories, textual accounts, and conversations as culturally and historically embedded ... [and] how narrative can serve to describe, construct, and transform a web of relationships" (Pachucki & Breiger, 2010: 209). This line of work resonates well with existing cultural entrepreneurship research, but also helps to situate individual identity work and processes of legitimation within broader field-wide narratives and relationships (see Wry, Lounsbury, & Glynn, 2011 for an initial move in this direction).

Works of interest here include those of Franzosi (1998) on narrative sequencing, Somers (1993) on the relationality of narrative, Bearman and colleagues on stories and identity (e.g., Bearman et al., 1999; Bearman & Parigi, 2004; Bearman & Stovel, 2000), and Seidel, Hannigan, and Phillips (forthcoming) on the study of social media and rumor communities.

Research on the duality of culture and networks in the context of fields, using varied relational methods, has been quite generative. For instance, Mohr and Guerra-Pearson (2010) show how the entrepreneurial efforts of community social welfare service agencies that (re)defined the status categories of welfare relief recipients facilitated the replacement of settlement houses with social work bureaucracies in the New York City social welfare field at the turn of the twentieth century. Drawing on the technique of multidimensional scaling, their analysis focused on the structuration of discursive status categories that organized welfare relief recipients such as men, women, boys, and girls; the classes of social problems encountered, such as criminality, delinquency, and disability; and technologies of organizational action, such as general relief, employment assistance, and character building.

In a similar vein, Ruef (1999) tracked changes in the discourse on organizational forms in the U.S. health care field after the passage of the 1965 Medicare and Medicaid Acts. He showed how logics of accessibility and quality shifted towards an emphasis on clinical and functional efficiency. Discursive data came from a systematic content analysis of over 32,000 texts from medical journals extracted from Medline. Drawing on map analysis (Carley, 1993) and multidimensional scaling techniques, Ruef was able to demonstrate how broad changes in discourse at the field level provided an opportunity for the social space of organizational forms and the status order of field participants to be transformed.

Mische and Pattison's (2000) analysis of the cultural and organizational dynamics underpinning the 1992 Brazilian impeachment of President Fernando Collor de Melo on corruption charges highlights how pro- or anti-impeachment organizational coalitions formed as a result of discursive positioning in the field of Brazilian politics. Drawing on discursive data including public relations materials, pamphlets, resolutions, and other organizational documents, they showed how a wide variety of organizational forms and the interconnections and alliances between them, and their discursive claims about the particular kinds of projects in which they were engaged, shaped the impeachment dynamic. Professional, religious, labor, nongovernmental, peak business, youth, political party, and state organizations were all implicated. Methodologically, galois lattice techniques

(Duquenne, 1991; Freeman & White, 1993) were employed to analyze the socio-cultural dynamics of the impeachment movement.

Meyer and Höllerer (2010) used in-depth content analysis with multivariate statistics, including correspondence analysis of actors and frames related to shareholder value in Austria, to uncover how competing logics undergirded and shaped the field of corporate governance in Austria. They developed a topographical map that highlighted the multidimensional space in which conflict between Continental European and Anglo-American models of corporate governance generated different identity positions for actors (e.g., politicians, trade unions, consultants, non-listed companies, listed corporations, securities analysts, investors). Their analysis showed that there was a strong link between the way in which actors interpret issues and their social positions in the field, highlighting the limits of more actor-centered approaches to meaning that neglect to situate actors and meanings in relation to each other. They argue that fields enable and constrain actors by providing a "menu of framings" in contrast to the more actor-centered imagery of accessing and deploying culture as if "dining à la carte" (Meyer & Höllerer, 2010: 1259).

More recent work has contemplated new ways to understand and measure culture (Mohr & Ghaziani, 2014). In particular, the possibility of harnessing "Big Data," and tools emanating from computer scientists and computational linguistics (e.g., topic modeling), have opened up new possibilities for the study of cultural processes (e.g., Bail, 2014; DiMaggio, Nag & Blei, 2013; Hannigan, 2015). Moreover, as new technologies have enabled virtual connections on social media via Facebook, Instagram, and Twitter, for instance, "relationships include those mediated by information technology . . . a world of imagined personal connections through some medium" (Cerulo 1997; Swidler 2001; cited in Lamont & Molnar, 2002). As a result, culture has emerged online as "people have come increasingly to conceive of themselves as members of very large collectivities linked primarily by common identities but minimally by networks of directly interpersonal relationships" (Calhoun, 1991: 95–96). The structuration of social ties fosters an "imagined community," which Anderson (1983: 5) describes as follows: "the members of even the smallest nation will never know most of their fellow-members, meet them, or even hear of them, yet in the minds of each lives the image of their communion" (Anderson, 1983: 5). Thus, communities, along with their embedded cultures, may be temporally bound, "homogeneous" in time by way of "consciousness of a shared temporal dimension in which they co-exist" (Anderson, 1983), and, in effect, constitute a field.

Nonetheless, key imagery that stems from these developments includes the conceptualization of fields as socio-cultural spaces that are comprised of variegated cultural resources, forms, and identities. This differentiated conception of fields, echoing Bourdieu, "gives us a way to incorporate maximal cultural context and generalizability in scientific explanation" (Pachucki & Breiger, 2010: 213; see also Martin, 2003). How cultural forms or identity positions get differentiated in a field draws attention to issues such as the making of symbolic and social boundaries (Lamont & Molnar, 2002). As we discuss in the next section, the study of boundaries that segregate cultural forms in a field (e.g., kinds of organizations, technologies, or products), and the "cultural holes" (Lizardo, 2014; Pachucki & Breiger, 2010) or interstitial spaces (Furnari, 2014; Rao, Morrill, & Zald, 2000) between such forms, may enable us to shed new light on, and redirect the study of, "entrepreneurial opportunities" – a core research topic in entrepreneurship upon which we elaborate in the next section, re-conceptualizing entrepreneurial opportunities as waxing and waning constellations of entrepreneurial possibilities in institutional fields.

To come full circle, we began this section by claiming that research on cultural entrepreneurship, even if focused on the identity stories of individual organizations and their consequences, should be situated in the context of institutional fields. This provides a key macrofoundational commitment for cultural entrepreneurship research that compels researchers to analyze individual actors in relationship to other actors in and around institutional fields. Although advancement of "new structural" methods (Lounsbury & Ventresca, 2003; Mohr, 1998) has provided an enhanced toolkit for cultural entrepreneurship research, we urge researchers to engage in a wider variety of key theoretical issues and questions related to the analysis of institutional fields. We have highlighted a number of theoretical research questions meriting further attention, including how fields emerge amidst a community ecology of fields, how actors come to be perceived as core members of a field, and how actors achieve optimal distinctiveness and higher performance or valuations in and around institutional fields. In the next sections, we build on these arguments by developing implications for the study of entrepreneurial possibilities.

4 Implications for the Study of Entrepreneurial Possibilities

Venkataraman (1997: 120) asserts that entrepreneurship research is centrally concerned with understanding "how opportunities to bring into existence 'future' goods and services are discovered, created, and exploited, by whom, and with what consequences" (see also Shane & Venkataraman, 2000). Given that entrepreneurship is still a relatively young field of research, our understanding of these processes remains limited. There is a longstanding economic tradition that conceptualizes wealth-creating opportunities as emerging from market disequilibria (e.g., Schumpeter 1939, Kirzner 1979). However, this conceptualization of entrepreneurial opportunities as exogenous accidents or competitive imperfections waiting to be discovered (Shane, 2003) has hindered the development of a richer understanding of how opportunities emerge and get exploited by entrepreneurs (Cornelissen & Clarke, 2010; McMullen & Shepherd, 2006).

Foss and Klein (2012) assert that research on entrepreneurial opportunities has been too narrowly focused on the psychological aspects of opportunity discovery, neglecting processes that link entrepreneurial perception to opportunity exploitation. McMullen, Plummer, and Acs (2007) argue that the concept of "entrepreneurial opportunity" itself remains vague as there is no consensus regarding what they are or where they come from. Companys and McMullen (2007: 303) suggest that "an entrepreneurial opportunity is more accurately described as an opportunity to engage in entrepreneurial action" – what we prefer to label as an "entrepreneurial possibility."

Recently, some scholars have begun to focus on how entrepreneurial opportunities are endogenously created, and how the creation of such opportunities has implications for how entrepreneurs exploit them (e.g., Aldrich & Ruef, 2006; Alvarez & Barney 2007, 2010; Alvarez, Barney, & Anderson, 2013). Although our emphasis is a bit different, we are sympathetic to this line of thinking as well as to more process-based or dynamic approaches to entrepreneurship (Brown & Eisenhardt, 1997; Chiles et al., 2010) and those that emphasize the importance of ongoing interactions between entrepreneurs and the communities in which they are embedded (Shepherd & Patzelt, 2017).

However, we take issue with those who have treated discovery and creation approaches to entrepreneurial opportunity as equally plausible explanatory alternatives; to us, this is akin to choosing one pack of gum from another. For example, Alvarez, Barney, and Anderson (2013: 308) argue that "some opportunities are not formed by exogenous shocks to preexisting markets or industries but instead are formed endogenously by the actions of those seeking to generate economic wealth themselves." They go on to suggest that empirical research on entrepreneurship could be usefully guided by questions such as, "Are opportunities objective and discovered, or are they enacted and created? Do the differences between entrepreneurs and nonentrepreneurs lead the former to discover and exploit opportunities of which the latter are not even aware, or are these differences – if they exist – the result of the process of creating opportunities rather than the cause of discovering opportunities?"

(Alvarez, Barney, & Anderson, 2013: 310). Setting aside the fact that ontological assumptions about the nature of reality cannot be adequately adjudicated by empirical evidence (Kuhn, 1970; Lakatos, 1978), the discovery-versus-creation debate threatens to reinvent the unhelpful structure-versus-agency dualism.

Given the amount of social science ink that has been spilled to develop much richer and balanced approaches to structure and agency (Bourdieu, 1977; Giddens, 1979; Sewell, 1992), it seems intellectually barren to contemplate whether entrepreneurial opportunities objectively exist, awaiting discovery by alert entrepreneurs (e.g., Shane 2003; Kirzner 1979), or are subjectively created (Alvarez et al. 2014; Garud and Giuliani 2013; Sarasvathy 2008). Giddens (1981: 27) has argued that "structure" is "both the medium and the outcome of the practices which constitute social systems." Building on Giddens, Sewell (1992: 4) opines that:

> structures shape people's practices, but it is also people's practices that constitute (and reproduce) structures. In this view of things, human agency and structure, far from being opposed, in fact presuppose each other. Structures are enacted by what Giddens calls "knowledgeable" human agents (i.e., people who know what they are doing and how to do it), and agents act by putting into practice their necessarily structured knowledge … This conception of human agents as "knowledgeable" and "enabled" implies that those agents are capable of putting their structurally formed capacities to work in creative or innovative ways. And, if enough people or even a few people who are powerful enough act in innovative ways, their action may have the consequence of transforming the very structures that gave them the capacity to act.

Bourdieu's corpus similarly focused on overcoming dualities of structure versus agency as well as objectivism versus subjectivism. Finding much to dislike in the 1950s' objectivism of Levi-Strauss and existentialism of Sartre, Bourdieu (1977) developed a theory of practice that sought to overcome these binary oppositions through a "structuralist constructivism or constructivist structuralism" (Bourdieu & Wacquant, 1992: 11). As signaled in the previous section, our approach to cultural entrepreneurship builds on these insights to forge an approach to *entrepreneurial possibilities* that overcomes the false choice between discovery and creation. In particular, we seek to advance our approach to entrepreneurship via an institutional field analysis that situates actors (including entrepreneurs, potential entrepreneurs, and organizations) in a cultural space of possibilities that provide constraints as well as resources for the emergence and demise of what the entrepreneurship literature has referred to as "opportunities." One might think about our approach as a cultural ecology of entrepreneurial possibilities, i.e., a system of interconnected options generated by the interaction of a community with its environment. To do so, we seek to define entrepreneurial possibilities at a collective level, rather than that of only individual entrepreneurs.

For instance, in highlighting the role of science in generating commercially oriented entrepreneurial opportunities, Sanders (2007) decomposes the entrepreneurial opportunity into various knowledge components that an entrepreneur brings together in novel combinations to create a product. We find this imagery attractive because it situates entrepreneurs in a broader relational field of knowledge where entrepreneurial opportunities are conceptualized as cultural elements that get defined by networks of knowledge or cultural authorities. However, we believe that Sanders accords entrepreneurs too much of a role; we alternatively conceptualize those networks of cultural elements that define entrepreneurial possibilities as collectively constructed and emergent, not created de novo by bold, visionary, or heroic entrepreneurs. In addition, although knowledge is a crucial kind of cultural element, we seek to broaden Sanders's emphasis on knowledge by emphasizing that it is not a free-floating resource but is situated within concrete communities of practice and identities (Duguid, 2005).

Thus, we propose the following:

Possibilities for entrepreneurial action exist at the interstices of distinct identity positions in and around institutional fields where novel entrepreneurial identities and practices may be constructed.

Ruef's (2000) community ecology approach to the study of organizational forms provides fruitful guidance for what we have in mind (see also Aldrich & Ruef, 2006). In his effort to explain the emergence of new organizational forms in the healthcare field, Ruef's analysis of MEDLINE discourse suggests that growing attention to common characteristics and issues undergirding a set of organization form identities by healthcare professionals can pave the way for the creation of new kinds of healthcare organizational forms. He shows how this is enabled by the existence of material infrastructure and the legitimacy of extant organizational forms (e.g., abortion clinics and family planning centers) that share an identity position in a field, but only up to a point. As the density of existing organizational forms for a particular identity position in a field becomes very high, it may dampen the overall effects of growing discourse that would enable new organizational form creation.

This conceptualization suggests that entrepreneurial possibilities can be understood as created by efforts to theorize the potential for new practices and identities (including new products and services) in the context of an existing relational identity space (i.e., an institutional field). That institutional field, constituted by various actors (organizations, entrepreneurs) and their identities, provides the context that both constrains and enables the imagination of existing actors and potential entrepreneurs as well as their efforts to theorize and assemble resources in the pursuit of entrepreneurial initiatives (Foss & Klein, 2012). As such, entrepreneurial possibilities can be said to be discursively constituted, and thus a precursor to actions such as the creation of new ventures that aim to benefit by exploiting a new possibility. But while there is potentially an infinite array of entrepreneurial possibilities that could be conceived, not anything is possible; entrepreneurial discourse is collectively shaped by the existing activities and beliefs held by actors in a field. In mature fields, this is reinforced by industry media, trade shows, and the like that constrain as well as enable what entrepreneurial possibilities are perceived as interesting and viable. In more mature fields, efforts to theorize more radical entrepreneurial possibilities may be difficult as proponents of radical innovations will bump into resistance grounded in power relationships tied to established ways of doing things (Harmon, Green, & Goodnight, 2015).

From a cultural entrepreneurship perspective, it is important to understand institutional fields as constituted by actors and discourse, and a key aspect of the construction of entrepreneurial possibilities occurs in the discursive dimension of fields. Thus conceived, entrepreneurial possibilities may be catalyzed by "cultural holes" (Lizardo, 2014; Pachucki & Breiger, 2010). Like structural holes (Burt, 1992) that refer to spaces between clusters of actors that provide entrepreneurial possibilities for network bridgers, cultural holes refer to interstitial spaces between relatively established or understood identities that provide entrepreneurial possibilities for the creation of new identities, or the expansion or editing of existing identities via cultural bridging or bricolage (Baker, Miner, & Eesley, 2003; Baker & Nelson, 2005). This involves temporal work by future-oriented change agents (i.e., entrepreneurs) that seek to convince various audiences of the merits of new kinds of activities (Kaplan & Orlokowski, 2013). A key mechanism by which this occurs is theorization (Strang & Meyer, 1992) or projective agency in the form of storytelling about what will, might, or should occur in the future (Emirbayer & Mische, 1998; Iddo, Tavory & Eliasoph, 2013; Mische, 2009, 2014; Rindova and Fombrun, 2001; van Werven, Bouwmeester, & Cornelissen, 2015).

For example, Martha Stewart built an empire with her varied cultural products – magazines, television shows, radio programs, newspaper columns, books, house and home items – by taking the ordinary things of life and weaving them together as one's lifestyle, thereby advancing a new, improved, and hip form of domesticity. This entrepreneurial possibility was made real via Stewart's flagship product, her magazine, expansively titled *Living*, which articulated her concept of lifestyle, with a reach that is extensive: "Beautiful soups and how to make them, beautiful houses and how to build them, beautiful children and how to raise them" (Glynn, 2011: 63). Stewart took the very ordinary and non-proprietary activities of living – cooking, vacuuming, ironing, gardening, decorating, and more generally home-keeping – and bundled together these disparate threads to weave a lifestyle, and one that was for sale. Martha Stewart centralized and condensed lifestyle into a package for which she could serve as a cultural authority and arbiter. In an early issue of the magazine (April–May 1994, Letter from Martha), she explains:

> *When I started this magazine in 1990, I felt it was essential to use my image as well as my name on every cover. Together, the image and the name formed a sort of "brand statement" that readers could quickly identify. At the time, I was best known for my series of books on food, entertaining, and lifestyle, and my picture was always prominently displayed on the jackets of those books for the same reason.*

As a cultural entrepreneur, Martha Stewart controlled her narrative, constructing and reconstructing her own story, the heart of which she claimed was like this: "I take the simple things of life and teach others how to do them, everyday things … [my goal] is to teach, to inform, and to inspire all of you in the preservation and extension of traditional family values and activities" (Stewart, 1997: 12).

In arguing for a focus on the constitutive nature of future-oriented discourse, rooted in pragmatist thought (Dewey, 1922; Mead, 1932; Schutz, 1951, 1967), Mische (2014: 441) claims that "future projections do not just happen inside people's heads, but rather develop via communicative interaction within groups, organizations, and institutional settings. Thus we need to focus on the effects of talk on future projections – not just in retrospective account-making, but in the jostling, jockeying, listening, learning, and arguing talk that unfolds in relational settings and is located in larger contentious fields." Stories of future projection "serve as maps for action and provide both motivation and orientation (i.e., moral, emotional, and practical guidance). Such narratives reduce complexity and persuade individuals and groups of the 'actionability' (i.e., desirability and feasibility) of particular lines of action" (Mische, 2014: 444; see also Ricoeur, 1991; Shackle, 1979). Of course, the relationship between prospective and retrospective is dynamic and needs to be analytically scrutinized (Scott & Lyman, 1968; Stokes & Hewitt, 1976)

Crucial to the explanation of entrepreneurial action is how stories related to entrepreneurial possibilities provide motivation. Although emotion has been a relatively neglected topic in entrepreneurial research (but see Baron, 2008; Cardon, Wincent, Singh, & Drnovsek, 2009; Cardon, Zietsma, Saparito, Matherne, & Davis, 2005; Shepherd, Patzelt, & Wolfe, 2011), it clearly plays a crucial role in the entrepreneurial process worthy of investigation (Shepherd & Patzelt, 2017). This has been stressed by social movement scholars who seek to explain how narrative frames facilitate collective mobilization (e.g., Benford & Snow, 1986; Polletta, 2006; Voss, 1998). A critically important future research direction is to engage the growing attention to values and emotion in organizational theory to further elaborate our theorization of cultural entrepreneurship processes (Gehman, Treviño, & Garud 2013; Harmon, 2018; Massa et al., 2017; Toubiana & Zietsma, 2017; Voronov, 2014; Voronov & Vince, 2012; Voronov & Weber, 2017; Zietsma & Toubiana, 2018).

The importance of emotion to cultural entrepreneurship is illustrated in the stories told by Martha Stewart in her magazine, *Martha Stewart Living*. From the inaugural issue of the magazine in 1990 to mid-2004, the time of Stewart's legal troubles, she authored two columns – "Letter" (from Martha) and "Remembering" (by Martha) – that bookended the magazine. In an analysis of these 253 columns, Glynn and Dowd (2008) coded them for the expression of positive and negative emotions. The range of emotions was dramatic, ranging from the euphoria associated with the "thrill" of MSLO's IPO success in 1999 to devastation, where Stewart conveyed how she was "sick to my heart" under the weight of the scandal in 2004 (Glynn & Dowd, 2008, p. 84). Overall, there was a fairly balanced expression of emotions by Stewart, but the extent of emotive discourse varied by both the format (the more personal and nostalgic "Remembering" was imbued with greater emotion) and by the performance context of the organization such that "Stewart voiced positive exuberance in years of struggle and muted that exuberance in years of expansion" (p. 89). Thus, emotionally laden discourse can figure in the narratives told by cultural entrepreneurs; importantly, as Glynn and Dowd (2008) demonstrated, it seems to reveal both a human and vulnerable side of the entrepreneur, especially when times are good, but can also blunt organizational decline and personal scandal.

In general, under conditions of extreme uncertainty (Knight, 1921), stories of the future aim to generate confidence in, and motivation for, various lines of action whether that involves decisions related to research and development investments made by multinational corporations or venture capital investments in new ventures (Wry, Lounsbury, & Glynn, 2011). "Stories provide causal links to show how the gap between the present state of the world and the predicted future state will be closed, thus providing plausible reasons why one should expect the outcome the teller has chosen to depict" (Beckert, 2016: 69). Below, we draw on the empirical case of nanotechnology to illustrate our cultural entrepreneurship approach to the study of entrepreneurial possibilities in institutional fields.

4.1 Entrepreneurial Possibilities in Nanotechnology: An Illustration

To concretize our analytical approach, we illustrate our ideas with an empirical example from nanotechnology. Over the past three decades, nanotechnology has emerged as an important area of scientific and commercial development. The prefix "nano" indicates that research and application are focused on innovations at the nanometer scale – a billionth of a meter (1/75,000th the width of a human hair). Nanotechnologies are typically located at less than 100 nanometers where materials can have unique properties (stronger, lighter, greater conductivity, etc.). Given that nanoscience is defined by inquiry into the very small, research occurs across a wide range of disciplines (e.g., chemistry, physics, biology) as well as in the medical sciences, engineering, and materials science.

While the publication of Eric Drexler's 1986 book, *Engines of Creation: The Coming Era of Nanotechnology*, is often referenced as a key catalyst for the emergence of the nanotechnology field, the development of atomic force microscopes and related equipment in the 1980s made systematic exploration at the nanoscale possible (Mody, 2011). This spurred scientific inquiry across a variety of disciplines and fields as well as practical efforts by entrepreneurs of all varieties to develop nanotechnologies and nanoproducts. In addition, many university scientists have been involved in technology development from the outset, making this a domain where basic and applied efforts were never distinct and separate realms. Although manipulation of atoms at the nano scale was seeded by the emergence of microscopy that could image at that level in the early 1980s, nanotechnology development was prominently accelerated with the National Nanotechnology Initiative (NNI) promulgated by President Clinton around the millennium.

Since then, nanotechnology patents and publications have grown exponentially, and efforts to commercialize various nanotechnologies have accelerated (Mody, 2011; Zucker, Darby, Furner, Liu, & Ma, 2007). For instance, the Woodrow Wilson International Center for Scholars Project on Emerging

Nanotechnologies has identified well over one thousand products that incorporate nanoscale silver, carbon, zinc, silicon/silica, titanium, or gold. Commercial applications resulting from nanotechnology have included the development of more durable tennis balls, lighter and stronger tennis rackets and golf clubs, stain-resistant clothing, and wear-resistant tires.

As an emerging area of scientific advance and technology development, possibilities for entrepreneurship are seemingly infinite. However, given scarce resources and limited time and attention, as well as variations in prior experience, not all entrepreneurial possibilities get developed and exploited equally (Eisenhardt & Schoonhoven, 1990). Given the vastness of nanotechnology, we zoom in on a crucial set of nanotechnology possibility spaces in the field of nanotubes, which include one of the most prominent nano inventions – carbon nanotubes (CNTs).

CNTs consist of graphitic layers seamlessly wrapped in a cylindrical shape and capped with pentagonal rings. They are extremely strong and have unique properties related to electrical and thermal conductivity, and optoelectronic transmission (Kroto et al., 1985). They are touted as having many times the strength of steel, the electrical conductivity of copper, and the narrow diameter of a DNA molecule. Applications for CNTs are wide ranging. Their unique electrical conducting properties have been shown to be useful in creating new kinds of diodes, transistors, probes, sensors, actuators, field emission arrays, and flat panel displays.

CNTs were forged out of discoveries beginning in the mid-1980s by Rice University chemist Richard (Rick) Smalley and several collaborators, who invented an entirely new form of carbon, in which the atoms were arranged as a tiny geodesic dome, labeled "buckminsterfullerene" after the architect who had popularized the shape. "With its neatly structured network of atoms, the 'buckyball' quickly became the poster molecule for nanotechnology" (MIT Technology Review, March 1, 2001). In 1996, Smalley received the Nobel Prize for his discoveries and became a prominent scientist in nanotechnology policy circles.

While CNTs are the most prominent kind of nanotube, there are other forms of nanotubes as we will discuss. However, even if we focus on CNTs, there is a wide array of possible applications and products that could be developed. In the early years of the nanotube field, there was an incredible amount of uncertainty about whether there was any entrepreneurial potential, and which possibilities might be most attractive.[2]

---

[2] Different aspects of the overall project we report on here can be found in Lounsbury, Wry, and Jennings (2010), Wry, Lounsbury, and Jennings (2014), Wry and Lounsbury (2013), Wry, Lounsbury, and Greenwood (2011), and Wry et al. (2010).

Drawing on an analysis of nanotube patents, we aim to illustrate the utility of a cultural entrepreneurship approach to the study of entrepreneurial possibilities in institutional fields. Following Kaplan and Vakili (2015), we conceptualize patents as cultural artifacts that may be treated analytically as texts. Although patents have been subject to various textual forms of analysis including bibliometrics (de Solla Price, 1965) and language analysis (e.g., Azoulay et al 2007; Yoon & Park 2005), Kaplan and Vakili (2015) interestingly employed topic modeling to analyze nanotechnology patent texts in order to determine the extent of their novelty. We build on this work, employing network analysis of patents over time as a way to understand the socio-cultural dynamics of institutional fields, including how actors and their identities are situated in relationship to each other, as well as to already identified and potential entrepreneurial possibilities. As research on patents and innovation has shown, commercial opportunities are often constructed by recombining existing and new knowledge (e.g., Grilliches, 1992; Jaffe, 1986; Jaffe and Trajtenberg, 2002). Based on the approach we outlined in the first part of this section, we conceptualize patent texts as a discursive corpus that maps out entrepreneurial possibilities that technology entrepreneurs may or may not pursue in the form of concrete commercial products in an effort to generate wealth.

Our analysis relies on all nanotube patents issued by the U.S. Patent Office (USPTO) from the initial patent in 1992 until the end of 2004 when the field had become more settled, cross-checked with NanoBank (see Zucker & Darby, 2007) to ensure comprehensiveness. Figure 3 plots the number of nanotube patents granted by year, showing that the issuance of patents was moderate and steady until around 2000 when the NNI was passed.

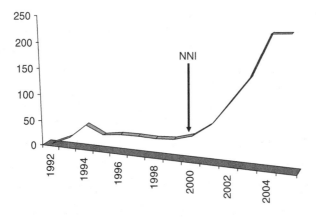

Figure 3 Nanotube Patents by Year

This dramatic rise of nanotube patenting prefigured many entrepreneurial possibilities. As a window into these possibilities, we analyzed the relational field of nanotube patents. The relationships between and among patents can be uncovered by tracking how they get classified by the United States Patent and Trademark Office (USPTO). The USPTO classification system aims to segregate one kind of technology from another based on similarities and differences in the central functions of underlying inventions. However, this is not so simple, and patents are typically assigned to a primary class as well as a number of secondary classes. These connections to other classes (i.e., other kinds of technologies) enable an analysis and understanding of how different inventions and kinds of technologies are relationally linked in a field.[3]

We conceptualize these relational linkages that wax and wane over time with the ongoing issuance of patents as an important signaling activity that prefigures potential entrepreneurial possibilities that might subsequently get commercially exploited (Sanders, 2007). This is consistent with studies that have used USPTO classes to differentiate between technological areas or communities of practice (e.g., Gilsing et al., 2008; Hall, Jaffe, & Trajtenberg, 2001; Rosenkopf & Nerkar, 2001), as well as applied patent analytical mapping used by entrepreneurs, corporations, and venture capitalists to evaluate white-space gaps where product innovation efforts may enable competitive advantage and wealth creation (e.g., Lux Venture Capital, 2006). It is important to emphasize that patents represent inventions that may or may not feed into the creation of new kinds of products and businesses, and so remain separate from the actual development of a product market. It is commonly estimated that "95 percent of all patented discoveries [are never] put to use to create new products and services, new jobs, and new economic growth" (Walker, 2015).

Drawing inspiration from new structuralist approaches to the study of culture mentioned in the preceding section (e.g., Bourdieu, 1984; DiMaggio, 1986; Lounsbury & Ventresca, 2003; Mische and Pattison, 2001; Mohr, 1998), we constructed a two-mode matrix of patents and the USPTO classes to which they were assigned. This enabled us to use network analytic techniques to analyze what network analysts refer to as joint involvement or affiliation data (e.g., Breiger 1974), using multidimensional scaling (MDS) to visually map how

---

[3] Note that although we rely on patent classification data to illustratively map the relational connections between and among entrepreneurial possibilities, the cross-classification of patents into secondary classes approximates other forms of textual analysis of patent text or bibliographic approaches to patent analysis. For instance, we have run bibliographic analyses of nanotube patent relationships, and the results are largely the same as reported here.

various USPTO patent classes were spatially related in the context of the nanotube field (Wasserman & Faust, 1997).[4] In the context of this illustration, patent classes (i.e., technology domains) that are more heavily linked via patent classification are plotted near each other while dissimilar classes are shown as spatially distant in an MDS plot.

Figure 4 shows the MDS plots of three-digit USPTO patent classes invoked by the nanotube patents we analyzed across four panels: 1994, 1998, 2001, and 2004. Not surprisingly, these plots show that the number of patent classes invoked grows over time; this is driven by growth in the scale and scope of nanotube patenting. Although connections between classes are sparse in 1994, over time, higher-density linkages between and across groups of classes enable clusters to form around more centrally invoked classes, while other classes become marginalized and even fall into disuse.

Results of hierarchical cluster analysis used in the generation of MDS plots show that two loose clusters began to form by 1998. These clusters highlight one of the big divides that occurred in the early development of the nanotube entrepreneurial opportunity space – that between organic and inorganic nanotubes (see Lounsbury, Wry, & Jennings, 2010). These distinct clusters are grounded in basic science inventions rooted in organic versus inorganic chemistry. The left side of the 1998 plot shows that entrepreneurial possibilities are being cultivated around an identity position defined by inorganic carbon nanotubes and various product-application areas including coatings and electrical systems. In the right side of the 1998 plot is a cluster of entrepreneurial possibilities being cultivated around organic nanotubes and product-application areas such as fuel compounds, synthetic resins, and other organic compounds.

Both identity position clusters around organic and inorganic nanotubes are still evident in 2001, although it is clear that there are growing entrepreneurial possibilities using inorganic nanotubes as more USPTO classes get absorbed into the cluster, while there appears to be shifting but also stagnating possibility development around organic nanotubes. In the inorganic nanotube cluster, new possibilities around semiconductors, active solid-state devices, and other kinds of electrical applications emerge – much of this is rooted in the growing validation and use of carbon nanotubes as a new nanoscale mechanism for electrical conductivity. On the organic side, there are new efforts to develop drug-related applications for nanotubes, while attention to fuels has diminished.

---

[4] Multidimensional scaling analyses generate visual representations based on an analysis of the Euclidean distances between entities analyzed (Kruskal & Wish, 1978).

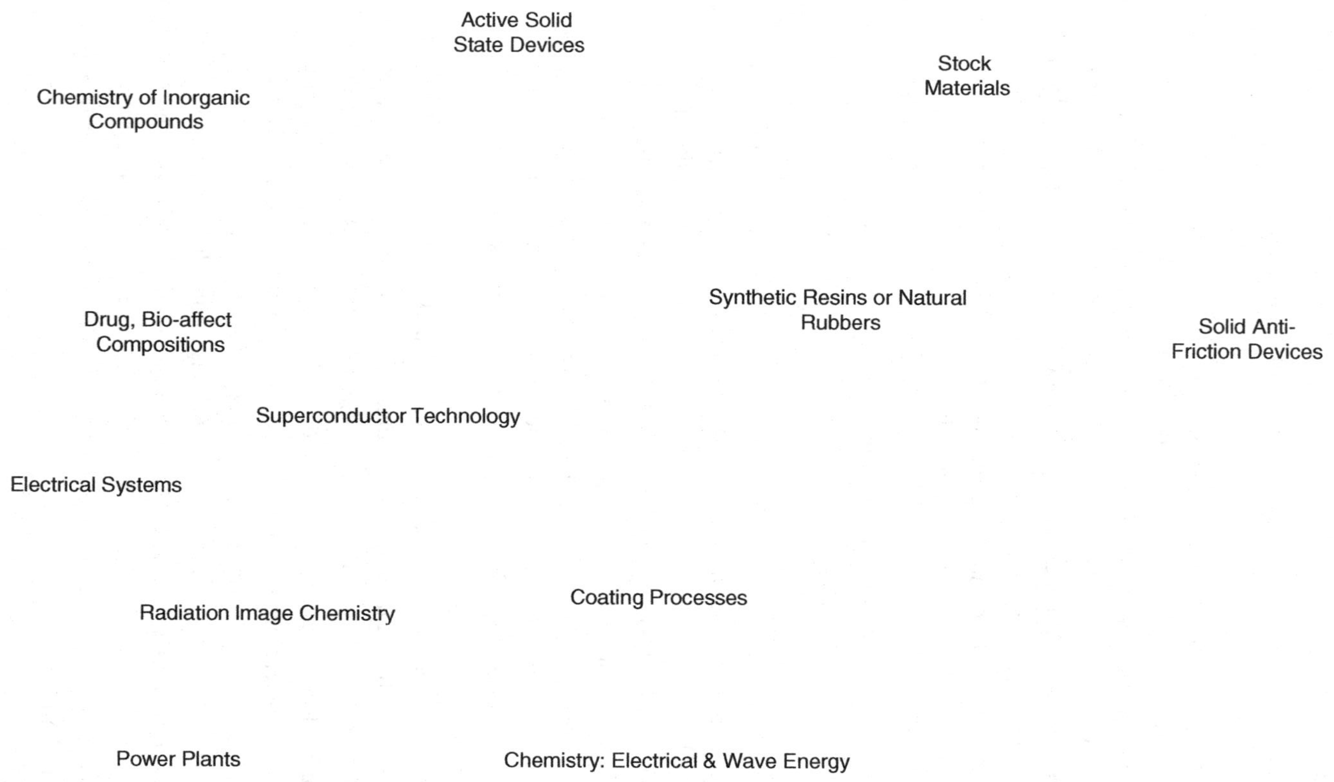

Chemistry of Inorganic
Compounds

Active Solid
State Devices

Stock
Materials

Solid Anti-
Friction Devices

Drug, Bio-affect
Compositions

Synthetic Resins or Natural
Rubbers

Superconductor Technology

Electrical Systems

Radiation Image Chemistry

Coating Processes

Power Plants

Chemistry: Electrical & Wave Energy

Figure 4a Entrepreneurial Possibilities in the Nanotube Field, 1994

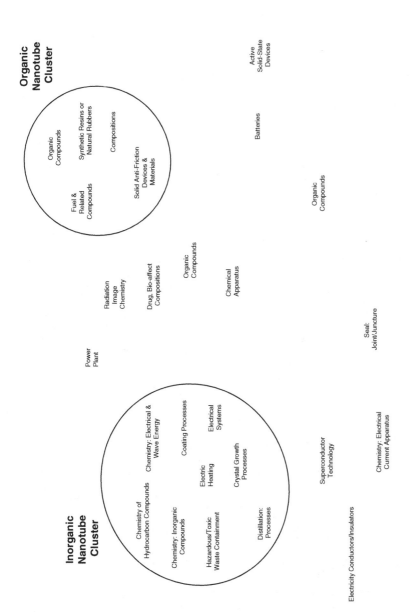

Figure 4b Entrepreneurial Possibilities in the Nanotube Field, 1998

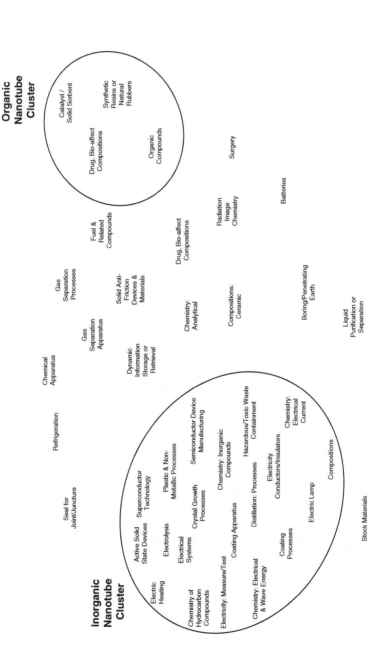

Figure 4c Entrepreneurial Possibilities in the Nanotube Field, 2001

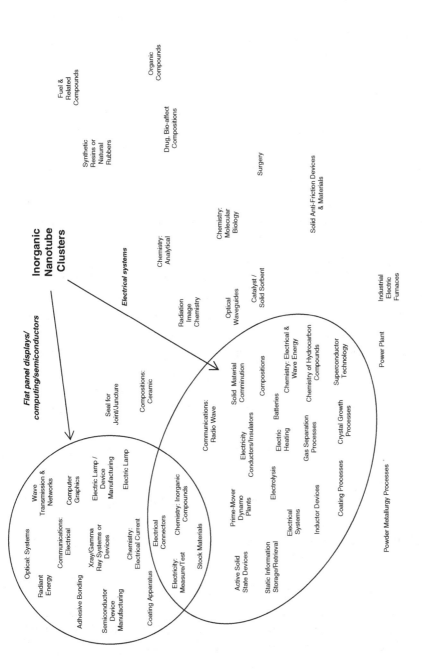

Figure 4d Entrepreneurial Possibilities in the Nanotube Field, 2004

By 2004, entrepreneurial possibilities involving organic nanotubes had been diminished further, and there is no longer a clustering of USPTO classes containing organic nanotube inventions. However, inventions involving inorganic, carbon nanotubes have expanded even further, and the 2001 inorganic nanotube cluster has begun to split, forming two overlapping clusters. In the upper left of the 2004 plot is a cluster of USPTO classes related to entrepreneurial possibilities in flat panel displays, computing, and semiconductors; below that is a cluster featuring other kinds of electrical systems.

Lounsbury, Wry, and Jennings (2010) discuss how entrepreneurial possibilities linked to inorganic nanotubes became more dominant and proliferated, focusing on the role of star scientist patenting and publishing activity as a key driver even though organic nanotube development was being promulgated by major corporations such as DuPont, Shell, and Exxon. They argued that star scientists such as Nobel Laureate Rick Smalley acted as cultural brokers (Hargadon & Sutton, 1997; Obstfeld, 2005) who actively promoted the generality of inorganic, carbon nanotubes by helping to pave a wide variety of, and interlinkages between, entrepreneurial opportunities in product application areas. They, in essence, created a community (Shepherd & Patzelt, 2017) around entrepreneurial possibility cultivation that enabled commercially oriented entrepreneurs and venture capitalists to commit risk capital in an effort to seize specific product-market opportunities signaled as promising by the discursive field of patents. In fact, in many cases, star scientists used their experience in cultivating these possibilities to create successful entrepreneurial ventures that accessed venture capital (e.g., Smalley created Carbon Nanotechnologies Inc.).

Lounsbury, Wry, and Jennings (2010) also provide evidence that the development of inorganic versus organic entrepreneurial possibilities had little to do with the inherent superiority of inorganic technologies or their applications. Through much of the 1990s, it appeared that inorganic and organic nanotubes provided entrepreneurial possibilities that seemed to have equal potential and support. The successful cultivation of inorganic versus organic nanotube possibilities occurred as a result of the development of an attractive narrative about the future, coupled with material developments in R&D and the creation of a robust community of practice, that, in a sense, began to mitigate the risk of commercial entrepreneurship. This increasingly resonant narrative helped to shift attention in the field towards the future potential of inorganic, carbon nanotubes – and this became manifest in the growth of patented inventions that we have tracked.

While a diverse array of actors and their communications fed into the future-oriented narrative of carbon nanotubes, this narrative was prominently cultivated and broadcasted by Nobel Laureate Rick Smalley, who also became a chief scientific advisor to the Clinton Administration in the construction of the National Nanotechnology Initiative. For instance, in a 2001 interview, Smalley exclaimed:

> I have to admit I'm just obsessed about carbon nanotubes. It's hard for me to go more than 10 minutes without talking about them. I think they are the coolest thing out there, and I think they'll have the greatest likely impact . . . In the nearest term, it looks like one application will be in [flat-panel] displays. A number of companies already have prototype displays using nanotubes. I won't be surprised if you see displays using nanotubes on the market within a few years. Another area that will be quick is as additives in engineering plastics [used in structural or high-tech applications like computer housing].

He went on to say:

> There is a "lunatic fringe" of the nanotube world that we haven't talked about yet . . . In theory you can make them to Alpha Centauri. What would be the strength of a long fiber? You would have the strongest damn thing ever made in the universe. Can we ever make that? And what good would it be? If you could make it cheaply and a continuous length, you could make the longest suspension bridge you ever heard about, *elevators in space* [Emphasis added]. (MIT Technology Review, March 1, 2001)

This narrative about near-term and science-fiction-like long-term scenarios (e.g., space elevators) for the development and use of carbon nanotubes was repeated and used as a model by the National Nanotechnology Initiative to promote future lines of development that not only resonated but inspired scientists and the general public. This included promising cures for cancer that target bad cells without killing good ones, providing potable water across the globe, and gee-whiz forms of quantum computing. Given Smalley's prominence as a scientist and Washington nanotechnology insider, his efforts and the resonance of this narrative also unlocked an incredible amount of government-directed resources that flowed into the ongoing scientific development of carbon nanotubes and related applications.

It is important to emphasize that while our analysis of entrepreneurial possibilities centers on the classification of issued patents, it was also importantly influenced by stories in scientific papers, scientific and technology media, and general talk at conferences and trade shows including those focused on the investment potential of nanotubes. A more comprehensive analysis of the cultural entrepreneurship of possibilities should investigate the relationship between various kinds of intersecting discourses that help direct attention towards some entrepreneurial possibilities versus others, helping to legitimate certain ideas about fruitful future developments that lead to commitments in the present. Of course, entrepreneurial possibility discourse also intersects with entrepreneurial action, and actual commitments to commercially pursue certain entrepreneurial possibilities have feedback effects on the entrepreneurial possibilities discourse. In the context of our illustration, the creation of new entrepreneurial ventures in inorganic, carbon nanotubes would play a key role in helping to solidify entrepreneurial possibilities related to inorganic nanotubes, and subsequent patenting and innovation focus on inorganic versus organic nanotubes.

Going back to our MDS plots of entrepreneurial possibilities rooted in patent classification, we conceptualize these images also as identity spaces for various actors. Given that patents are assigned to particular actors, whether that is a corporation, university, government agency, or individual inventor, these various actors underlie entrepreneurial possibility creation and become identified with them (Podolny & Stuart, 1995). For instance, major corporations including DuPont, Shell, and Exxon were issued a number of organic nanotube patents. And since they had no inorganic nanotube patents, their identities in the field of nanotube entrepreneurial possibilities would be associated more exclusively with organic nanotubes. In contrast, inorganic nanotube patents were issued to a variety of universities such as Rice, Northwestern, and Harvard as well as corporations active in computing such as IBM and in electronics such as Samsung. Thus, a more comprehensive field mapping could overlay actors onto the identity space created by entrepreneurial possibility discourse.

By doing so, we may connect the study of entrepreneurial possibilities to the cultural entrepreneurship of specific organizations or entrepreneurs and their efforts to establish optimally distinctive identity positions. Of course, patents held by organizations, especially high technology start-ups, become core touchstones for their identity and how they are understood both internally and externally. An organization's patent portfolio is often referenced and discussed on their website, and drawn upon by media and analysts who are evaluating or writing stories about an organization. It is no surprise that actors whose identity is associated strongly with particular entrepreneurial possibilities may help us understand which actors are more likely to actual try to seize upon those possibilities. Thus, cultural entrepreneurship is dynamically unfolding across multiple levels as actors try to establish optimally distinctive identities in and across an ambiguous and ever-changing institutional field of entrepreneurial possibilities. The conventional focus on entrepreneurial opportunity – that is, the specific possibilities that get developed and from which entrepreneurs make money – largely brackets these broader contextual dynamics within which power, politics, and even dumb luck provide core elements that influence the production of "entrepreneurial opportunities."

While we have discussed nanotube possibilities in the broad groupings of organic versus inorganic applications, we can also zoom in on specific entrepreneurial possibilities to understand their particular fates. That is, although it is useful to highlight the growth of inorganic versus organic nanotube possibilities, we can also identify the rise and fall of more specific inorganic entrepreneurial possibilities, and the entrepreneurial firms that seek to exploit them. When we do so, understanding the relational connections among different bits of knowledge and their associated communities of practice becomes even more critical. Harkening back to our theoretical discussion of the new structuralism in the previous section, it is useful to think about the spatial gaps between entrepreneurial possibilities (three-digit USPTO classes in our MDS plots) as *cultural holes* that constrain and enable the cultivation of entrepreneurial possibilities.

In scanning the various knowledge domains identified and how they change over time, one can see that some shift from more marginal to more central positions, highlighting how cultural holes between knowledge domains get bridged and form new entrepreneurial possibilities. For instance, in 1998, the knowledge domain involving "active solid-state devices" remained marginal, outside of the two key inorganic and organic entrepreneurial possibility clusters. However, by 2000, this knowledge domain had shifted to become part of the core cluster of inorganic nanotube entrepreneurial possibilities.

In the context of the field of nanotubes, this means that nanotube patents classified in "active solid-state devices" became increasingly cross-classified in other knowledge domains that became central to the emerging cluster of possibilities – for example, "chemistry of inorganic compounds" and "coating processes." The bridging of such cultural holes that make certain knowledge domains more central involves the active efforts of inventors who are seeking to make such connections by expanding the range of applications to which nanotubes are relevant. For instance, famous nanoscience pioneer Charles Lieber (Northwestern University), who had already gained considerable acclaim for his work in active solid-state devices (high-temperature semiconductors), sought to bridge his work in that area to emerging developments in nanotechnology. In a 2003 interview, he detailed his entry into nanotube research: "With my work on high temperature semiconductors, I had been studying quasi-two-dimensional planar structures ... Also, at the same time, interesting work was going on with fullerenes and carbon nanotubes ... nanowires were going to be absolutely essential and I figured I might as well go for it" (Lieber, 2003: 2).

It is through such cultural bridging of knowledge domains by individual inventors that core clusters of entrepreneurial possibilities form and new entrepreneurial possibilities gain in visibility and interest. By conceptualizing entrepreneurial possibilities in this way, broken down into cultural components (e.g., knowledge domains) of an interlinked innovation ecosystem, the identities of actors (i.e., entrepreneurs, corporations) in such an institutional field can be understood by how they span different knowledge domains. Like French chefs who cultivate hybrid identities that result from offering various mixes of haute and nouvelle cuisine dishes (Rao et al., 2005), nanotechnology entrepreneurs cultivate their identities in the nanotube field as a result of their innovative bricolage across patent classes (i.e., knowledge domains). However, the identities entrepreneurs cultivate in an institutional field not only shape (in aggregate) whether entrepreneurial possibilities rise or fall in visibility and attractiveness, but can have an impact on the ultimate success of an entrepreneur as well. As indicated by Wry and Lounsbury (2013) and Wry, Lounsbury, and Jennings (2014), nanotube start-ups are more likely to be funded by venture capitalists when their identities span knowledge domains that are perceived as symbiotic – in this case, often effectively bridging science and technology knowledge domains.

With respect to inorganic carbon nanotubes, this often involved bridging novel developments in basic science, frequently involving new ways to synthesize carbon nanotubes (represented by platform patents in inorganic chemistry and compositions), and commercial application opportunities such as flat panel displays and computers. Venture capitalists emphasized the value they found in identities that bridged scientific and technological possibilities (quoted in Wry, Lounsbury, and Jennings, 2014: 1314):

> *I love companies that have downstream [product focused] IP that validates fundamental process and material patents ... it shows me that they're getting serious and thinking about how they're going to impact the big market that their discovery relates to.*
>
> *Science moving to technology makes firms attractive ... it hits the boxes that the VCs want you to tick ... you need to demonstrate the feasibility of science for market applications.*

However, we need much more research on these kinds of cultural entrepreneurship processes. While our MDS plot of entrepreneurial possibilities provides some illustrative insight into the shifting nature of knowledge domains and entrepreneurial possibilities over time, and help to situate the identity of actors, it does not offer a general explanation of how entrepreneurial possibilities themselves got created and seized, and by whom with what consequences. But what we do hope our illustration has shown is that entrepreneurial possibilities can be studied as a field that is relatively distinct although intimately connected to entrepreneurial action that seeks to exploit entrepreneurial possibilities. Our illustration has also shown that entrepreneurial possibilities are best conceptualized as culturally constructed, and that cultural data related to stories, categories, and other cultural forms may be used to help us understand the process by which entrepreneurial possibilities emerge as a result of distributed, collective action.

Finally, we have emphasized that entrepreneurial possibilities cannot be understood and analyzed by focusing narrowly on discrete, individual-level possibilities. From our perspective, entrepreneurial possibilities must be understood as part of a field of action where there is an ever-evolving ecology of entrepreneurial possibilities, as well as a wide variety of potential and actual entrepreneurs, and other actors, who are variously involved in the construction and exploitation of possibilities. Such a dynamic, contextualized approach to cultural entrepreneurship promises much insight, and would invigorate not only our understanding of entrepreneurial processes, but also strategic management efforts to establish optimal distinctiveness to enhanced performance under conditions of a constantly shifting terrain. We believe that research in this direction could usefully expand the scope of cultural entrepreneurship research while also contributing to a more comprehensive understanding of how contextual dynamics shape entrepreneurial processes.

5 Conclusion: A New Agenda for the Study of Entrepreneurial Processes and Possibilities

It has been nearly two decades since we articulated our theory of cultural entrepreneurship. Writing this Element has afforded us an incredible opportunity to reflect on our theorization, as well as its evolution, elaboration, and impact over these years. Looking back, we recall our initial objective: to draw attention to "the dynamics of culture and symbolic activities" that entrepreneurs use to fuel the formation, growth, and legitimation of their nascent ventures (Lounsbury & Glynn, 2001: 548). To us, a significant missing piece in explaining the puzzle that is entrepreneurship was "culture" and we sought to redress this. In our 2001 formulation, we conceptualized culture as a resource available to entrepreneurs. In doing so, we built on Swidler's (1986) insightful "toolkit" approach to culture, i.e., as a set of available symbols, meanings, and explanations that could be appropriated by entrepreneurs to narrate, rationalize, and make convincing the potential of their new venture. Thus, we explicitly linked entrepreneurial activity and wealth creation to the astute use of culture – especially via entrepreneurial storytelling. Thus, one of our key aims was to reinforce an understudied connection between strategic and institutional perspectives in organization theory by conceptualizing entrepreneurs as "skilled cultural operatives" (559), capable of tapping cultural resources in the service of firm identity construction, legitimation, and resource acquisition.

Our initial cultural entrepreneurship framework had an allure because it made culture and cultural processes central to an understanding of entrepreneurship – a research domain dominated by an economic lens that has marginalized the role of culture (Foss, Klein, & Bjørnskov, forthcoming). Although there is a rich historical legacy of entrepreneurial research that has embraced culture and more interdisciplinarity (e.g., Aldrich & Ruef, 2006; Gartner, Bird, & Starr, 1992), the entrepreneurship field of study has become even more economically oriented, as exemplified in the narrow contemporary focus on entrepreneurial opportunities and discovery (Foss & Klein, 2012; Shane & Venkataraman, 2000; Venkataraman, 1997). However, underlying this mainstream pathos, a robust stream of research on cultural entrepreneurship has been building.

As we detailed, research on cultural entrepreneurship, at this point in time, has a rich legacy and is wide-ranging, although a great deal of research that built on our original paper (Lounsbury & Glynn, 2001) has hewed closely to our initial focus on story-telling and the legitimation of new entrepreneurial ventures (Überbacher, 2014). Although this line of scholarship has been extremely productive, we believe that it has only scratched the surface of the research agenda we outlined. Thus, in this Element, we sought to elaborate on key aspects of that agenda, highlighting key questions and issues that remain understudied. In addition, we engaged recent developments in cultural studies and organization theory to lay the foundations for a broader research agenda that could expand the scope of cultural entrepreneurship scholarship. As part of this effort, we discussed the implications of our expanded agenda for the study of entrepreneurial possibilities in institutional fields as a way to reorient narrow, economic discussions of entrepreneurial opportunity and discovery that dominate contemporary entrepreneurship research. In doing so, we seek to elevate the study of culture and cultural processes in entrepreneurship, and to encourage a return to a more cosmopolitan, interdisciplinary orientation towards the understanding of entrepreneurial processes.

Earlier in this Element (see section 2), we revisited our initial cultural entrepreneurship framework and highlighted two key mechanisms central to the model and to story-telling – identity formation and cultural resonance. In a sense, as we originally argued, story-telling was conceived as both a dependent and independent variable. As a dependent variable, story-telling is an outcome of processes of capital appropriation related to entrepreneurial identity formation; as an independent variable, story-telling is an antecedent to the acquisition of legitimacy, resource acquisition, and wealth creation from key stakeholders and audiences. To enhance our understanding of identity stories as outcomes, we highlighted the need to engage current developments at the interface of the institutional and identity literatures to cultivate a richer understanding of how individual entrepreneurial stories get constructed. This involves engaging new theoretical developments related to cultural process such as those in the institutional logics perspective that seeks to explain cultural heterogeneity in contrast to older institutional formulations emphasizing cultural homogeneity, or isomorphism, as a key trope (Thornton, Ocasio, & Lounsbury, 2012). To develop a richer understanding of how stories may enhance legitimacy and resource acquisition, we encouraged research that engages theory on cultural resonance and framing (Cornelissen & Werner, 2014; Giorgi, 2017: 712) to enrich explanations of how and why stories become appealing and convincing.

This line of theorization led us to firmly contextualize entrepreneurship, particularly within institutional fields; this is our main focus in section 3. Institutional fields afford a wealth of cultural materials that entrepreneurs can appropriate for crafting stories; they also serve as guard rails for defining identities that are optimally distinctive within that field. Moreover, institutional fields also furnish critical touchstones for cultural resonance, by recognizing the cognitive and emotional bases undergirding the relational structures among actors in a field. Drawing on contemporary social theory, and related developments in institutional analysis and the study of culture, we argued for the fruitfulness of expanding the scope of cultural entrepreneurship research. In developing a focus on contextual dynamics, we argued that cultural entrepreneurship occurs at multiple levels – from the individual entrepreneur to distributed, collective action in and across institutional fields that helps to shape a continually evolving space of entrepreneurial identities and possibilities.

A key aspect of research on optimal distinctiveness research has focused on a two-stage evaluation process of individual entrepreneurs and organizations – the first stage involves audience perceptions of an organization as a legitimate member of a particular field; the second stage has to do with audience evaluations of that organization relative to peers in the same field (Zuckerman, 2017). Although we need more research on both stages, most research attention has been given to the second stage, rather than the first (Zhao et al., 2017). Drawing on relational thinking (e.g., Bourdieu 1977, 1984; Emirbayer, 1997; Pachucki

& Breiger, 2010), we argued that more attention needs to be paid to how entrepreneurs and organizations try to position themselves in desired fields (possibly through their stories), and how audiences, in turn, perceive and evaluate the appropriateness of that positioning, in and across institutional fields. This involves not only individual or organizational acts of cultural entrepreneurship, but forms of cultural entrepreneurship that aim to configure and reconfigure bundles of meanings and practices that situate identity positions in and across institutional fields.

In section 4, we sought to make the more abstract arguments from section 3 more tangible, focusing on their implications for the study of entrepreneurial opportunities – what we relabel as entrepreneurial possibilities – as a way to avoid the baggage that makes current conversations of opportunity problematic. We highlight the need to disentangle fields of entrepreneurial possibilities from more concrete fields of established identities and practices. Current theory and research on entrepreneurial opportunity conflate the two when, in fact, entrepreneurial initiatives often take advantage of many prior efforts of other actors that make focal entrepreneurial initiatives conceivable in the first place. We drew on the case of nanotechnology patents and related entrepreneurship to illustrate the potential of our arguments and agenda.

Overall, we believe that cultural entrepreneurship research has the potential to make an important impact on the entrepreneurship research field by more strongly interconnecting the study of entrepreneurship with the fields of strategy and organization studies. In addition to re-conceptualizing and redirecting the study of entrepreneurial opportunities, we believe it is important to harness different strands of culturally sensitive research to develop a more synthetic conversation of how culture shapes entrepreneurial processes. Going beyond a focus on stories, our understanding of entrepreneurship can be considerably enhanced by understanding how various cultural resources related to discourse, logics, frames, routines, and, more generally, symbolism can be accessed and utilized in the pursuit of entrepreneurial initiatives. And we must seek to develop generalizable knowledge by expanding our research beyond high-growth commercial ventures to appreciate how cultural entrepreneurship works in a wide variety of situations including corporations, social enterprises, and state agencies. As we expand the scope of what we study empirically, the implications of this research agenda expand well beyond entrepreneurship and organization theory to include core issues of strategic management and social innovation.

References

Abrahamson, E., & Baumard, P. 2008. What lies behind organizational façades and how organizational façades lie: An untold story of organizational decision making. *The Oxford Handbook of Organizational Decision Making*, pp. 437–452.

Ahl, H. 2006. Why research on women entrepreneurs needs new directions. *Entrepreneurship Theory and Practice*, 30(5), pp. 595–621.

Albert, S., & Whetten, D. A. 1985. Organizational identity. In L. L. Cummings & B. M. Staw, eds. *Research in Organizational Behavior*. Greenwich, CT: JAI Press, Inc., pp. 263–295.

Aldrich, H. E. 2012. The emergence of entrepreneurship as an academic field: A personal essay on institutional entrepreneurship. *Research Policy*, 41: 1240–1248.

Aldrich, H. E., & Fiol, C. M. 1994. Fools rush in? The institutional context of industry creation. *Academy of Management Review*, 19(4), pp. 645–670.

Aldrich, H. E., & Ruef, M. 2006. *Organizations Evolving*, SAGE Publications. Available at: https://books.google.com/books?id=PIWJf4l5eMsC.

Aldrich, H. E., & Waldinger, R. 1990. Ethnicity and entrepreneurship. *Annual Review of Sociology*, 16(1), pp. 111–135.

Aldrich, H. E., & Wiedenmayer, G. 1993. From traits to rates: An ecological perspective on organizational foundings. *Advances in Entrepreneurship, Firm Emergence, and Growth*, 1(3), pp. 145–196.

Aldrich, H. E., & Zimmer., C. 1986. Entrepreneurship through social networks. In D. Sexton & R. Smilor, eds. *The Art and Science of Entrepreneurship*. New York: Ballinger, pp. 3–23. Available at: www.unc.edu/~healdric/Publ.pdf.

Alexander, J. C. 2003. *The Meanings of Social Life: A Cultural Sociology*. Oxford, UK: Oxford University Press.

Alvarez, S. A., et al. 2014. Realism in the study of entrepreneurship. *Academy of Management Review*, 39(2), pp. 227–231.

Alvarez, S. A., & Barney, J. B. 2010. Entrepreneurship and epistemology: The philosophical underpinnings of the study of entrepreneurial opportunities. *Academy of Management Annals*, 4(1), pp. 557–583.

2007. The entrepreneurial theory of the firm. *Journal of Management Studies*, 44(7), pp. 1057–1063.

Alvarez, S. A., Barney, J. B., & Anderson, P. 2013. Forming and exploiting opportunities: The implications of discovery and creation processes for entrepreneurial and organizational research. *Organization Science*, 24(1), pp. 301–317.

Ansari, S. M., Fiss, P. C., & Zajac, E. J. 2010. Made to fit: How practices vary as they diffuse. *Aademy of Management Review*, 35(1), pp. 67–92.

Arrow, K. J. 1983. Innovation in large and small firms. In *Entrepreneurship*. Lexington, MA: Lexington Books, pp. 15–28.

Ashforth, B. E., & Humphrey, R. H. 1997. The ubiquity and potency of labeling in organizations. *Organization Science*, 8(1), pp. 43–58.

Askin, N., & Mauskapf, M. 2017. What makes popular culture popular?: Product features and optimal differentiation in music. *American Sociological Review* 82, pp. 910–944.

Azoulay, P., Ding, W., & Stuart, T. 2007. The determinants of faculty patenting behavior: Demographics or opportunities? *Journal of Economic Behavior & Organization*, 63(4), pp. 599–623.

Bail, C. A. 2014. The cultural environment: Measuring culture with big data. *Theory and Society*, 43(3–4), pp. 465–482.

Baker, T., Miner, A. S., & Eesley, D. T. 2003. Improvising firms: Bricolage, account giving and improvisational competencies in the founding process. *Research Policy*, 32(2), pp. 255–276.

Baker, T., & Nelson, R. E. 2005. Creating something from nothing: Resource construction through entrepreneurial bricolage. *Administrative Science Quarterly*, 50(3), pp. 329–366.

Balogun, J., & Johnson, G. 2004. Organizational restructuring and middle manager sensemaking. *Academy of Management Journal*, 47(4), pp. 523–549. Available at: http://search.ebscohost.com/login.aspx?direct=true&db=bth&AN=14438585&site=bsi-live.

Barney, J., 1991. Firm resources and sustained competitive advantage. *Journal of Management*, 17(1), pp. 99–120.

Baron, R. A. 1998. Cognitive mechanisms in entrepreneurship: Why and when enterpreneurs think differently than other people. *Journal of Business Venturing*, 13(4), pp. 275–294.

2008. The role of affect in the entrepreneurial process. *Academy of Management Review*, 33(2), pp. 328–340.

Barry, D., & Elmes, M. 1997. Strategy retold: Toward a narrative view of strategic discourse. *Academy of Management Review*, 22(2), pp. 429–452.

Battilana, J., Leca, B., & Boxenbaum, E. 2009. How actors change institutions: Towards a theory of institutional entrepreneurship. *Academy of Management Annals*, 3, pp. 65–107.

Baumol, W. J. 1983. Toward operational models of entrepreneurship. In *Entrepreneurship*, pp. 29–47.

Bearman, P., Faris, R., & Moody, J. 1999. Blocking the future: New solutions for old problems in historical social science. *Social Science History*, 23(4), pp. 501–533.

Bearman, P., & Parigi, P. 2004. Cloning headless frogs and other important matters: Conversation topics and network structure. *Social Forces*, 83(2), pp. 535–557.

Bearman, P. S., & Stovel, K. 2000. Becoming a Nazi: A model for narrative networks. *Poetics*, 27(2–3), pp. 69–90.

Beckert, J. 2016. *Imagined Futures*. Harvard University Press.

Bennis, W. 1996. *On Becoming a Leader*. Pearson Education Canada.

Berger, P. L., & Luckmann, T. 1967. *The Social Construction of Reality*. Garden City, NY: Doubleday.

Boje, D. M. 1991. The storytelling organization: A study of story performance in an office-supply firm. *Administrative Science Quarterly*, pp. 106–126.

Borgatti, S. P., Jones, C., & Everett, M. G. 1998. Network measures of social capital. *Connections*, 21(2), pp. 27–36.

Bourdieu, P. 1977. *Outline of a Theory of Practice*. Cambridge, UK: Cambridge University Press.

1983. The field of cultural production or: the economic world reversed. In R. Johnson, ed. *The Field of Cultural Production: Essays on Art and Literature*. Cambridge: Polity Press, pp. 29–73.

1984. *Distinction: A Social Critique of the Judgement of Taste*. Cambridge, MA: Harvard University Press.

1990. *The Logic of Practice*. Stanford, CA: Stanford University Press.

1998. *Practical Reason*. Stanford, CA: Stanford University Press.

2000. *Pascalian Meditations*. Stanford University Press.

2007. *Sketch for a Self-Analysis*. Chicago, IL: University of Chicago Press.

Bourdieu, P., & Wacquant, L. J. D. 1992. *An Invitation to Reflexive Sociology*. University of Chicago Press.

Boxenbaum, E., & Jonsson, S. 2008. Isomorphism, diffusion and decoupling. *The Sage Handbook of Organizational Institutionalism*, pp. 78–98.

Breiger, R. L. 1974. The duality of persons and groups. *Social Forces*, 53(2), pp. 181–190.

Breiger, R. L., & Mohr, J. W. 2004. Institutional logics from the aggregation of organizational networks: Operational procedures for the analysis of counted data. *Computational & Mathematical Organization Theory*, 10(1), pp. 17–43.

Brewer, M. B. 1991. The social self: On being the same and different at the same time. *Personality and Social Psychology Bulletin*, 17(5), pp. 475–482. Available at: https://doi.org/10.1177/0146167291175001.

Brown, A. D., Gabriel, Y., & Gherardi, S. 2009. Storytelling and change: An unfolding story. *Organization*, 16(3), pp. 323–333.

Brown, S. L., & Eisenhardt, K. M. 1997. The art of continuous change: Linking complexity theory and time-paced evolution in relentlessly shifting organizations. *Administrative Science Quarterly*, pp. 1–34.

Bruner, J. 1991. The narrative construction of reality. *Critical Inquiry*, 18(1), pp. 1–21.

Burt, R. S. 1992. *Structural Holes: The Social Structure of Competition*. 1995 Issue. Harvard University Press.

Byron, C. M. 2002. *Martha, Inc.* New York: John Wiley & Sons, Inc.

Cardon, M. S., et al. 2005. A tale of passion: New insights into entrepreneurship from a parenthood metaphor. *Journal of Business Venturing*, 20(1), pp. 23–45.

2009. The nature and experience of entrepreneurial passion. *Academy of Management Review*, 34(3), pp. 511–532.

Carley, K. 1993. Coding choices for textual analysis: A comparison of content analysis and map analysis. *Sociological Methodology*, pp. 75–126.

Chiles, Todd H., Christopher S. Tuggle, Jeffery S. McMullen, Leonard Bierman, and Daniel W. Greening. 2010. Dynamic creation: Extending the radical Austrian approach to entrepreneurship. *Organization Studies* 31 (1). SAGE Publications Sage UK: London, England: 7–46.

Cliff, J. E., Langton, N., & Aldrich, H. E. 2005. Walking the talk? Gendered rhetoric vs. action in small firms. *Organization Studies*, 26(1), pp. 63–91.

Cochran, T. C. 1949. Role and sanction in American entrepreneurial history. In A. H. Cole, ed., *Change and the Entrepreneur: Postulates and Patterns for Entrepreneurial History*. Boston, MA: Harvard Business School Press, pp. 153–175.

Companys, Y. E., & McMullen, J. S. 2007. Strategic entrepreneurs at work: the nature, discovery, and exploitation of entrepreneurial opportunities. *Small Business Economics*, 28(4), pp. 301–322.

Cook, M. L., & Burress, M. J. 2009. A cooperative life cycle framework. In *International Conference "Rural Cooperation in the 21st Century: Lessons from the Past, Pathways to the Future,"* June, pp. 15–17.

Cornelissen, J. P., & Clarke, J. S. 2010. Imagining and rationalizing opportunities: Inductive reasoning and the creation and justification of new ventures. *The Academy of Management Review*, pp. 539–557.

Cornelissen, J. P., Haslam, S. A., & Balmer, J. M. T. 2007. Social identity, organizational identity and corporate identity: Towards an integrated understanding of processes, patternings and products. *British Journal of Management*, 18(s1).

Cornelissen, J. P., Holt, R., & Zundel, M., 2011. The role of analogy and metaphor in the framing and legitimization of strategic change. *Organization Studies*, 32(12), pp. 1701–1716.

Cornelissen, J. P., & Werner, M. D. 2014. Putting framing in perspective: A review of framing and frame analysis across the management and organizational literature. *Academy of Management Annals*, 8(1), p.181 LP-235. Available at: http://annals.aom.org/content/8/1/181.abstract.

Creed, W. E. D., Scully, M. A., & Austin, J. R. 2002. Clothes make the person? The tailoring of legitimating accounts and the social construction of identity. *Organization Science*, 13(5), pp. 475–496.

Czarniawska, B., 1997. *Narrating the Organization: Dramas of Institutional Identity*, University of Chicago Press.

Czarniawska, B., & Wolff, R. 1998. Constructing new identities in established organization fields: Young universities in old Europe. *International Studies of Management & Organization*, 28(3), pp. 32–56.

Dalpiaz, E., & Cavotta, Forthcoming. A double-edged sword: Cultural entrepreneurship and the mobilization of morally tainted cultural resources. *Innovation: Organization and Management*.

Deephouse, D. L. 1996. Does isomorphism legitimate? *Academy of Management Journal*, 39(4), pp. 1024–1039.

1999. To be different, or to be the same? It's a question (and theory) of strategic balance. *Strategic Management Journal*, 20(2), pp. 147–166. Available at: http://dx.doi.org/10.1002/(SICI)1097–0266(199902)20:2%3C147::AID-SMJ11%3E3.0.CO.

Deephouse, D. L., & Suchman, M. 2008. Legitimacy in organizational institutionalism. In R. Greenwood et al., eds., *The Sage Handbook of Organizational Institutionalism*. Beverly Hills, CA: Sage Publications, pp. 49–77.

Dewey, J., 1922. *Human Nature and Conduct: An Introduction to Social Psychology*, Carlton House.

DiMaggio, P. J. 1987. Classification in art. *American Sociological Review*, 52(4), pp. 440–455.

1982. Cultural entrepreneurship in nineteenth-century Boston: The creation of an organizational base for high culture. *Media, Culture and Society*, 4, pp. 33–50.

1986. Cultural entrepreneurship in nineteenth century Boston. In P. J. DiMaggio, ed. *Non-Profit Enterprise in the Arts: Studies in Mission and Constraint*. New York: Oxford University Press, pp. 41–61.

1997. Culture and cognition. *Annual Review of Sociology*, pp. 263–287.

1988. Interest and agency in institutional theory. In L. G. Zucker, ed., *Institutional Patterns and Organizations*. Cambridge, MA: Ballinger, pp. 3–22.

1991. Constructing an organizational field as a professional project: US art museums, 1920–1940. In W. W. Powell & P. J. DiMaggio, eds., *The New Institutionalism in Organizational Analysis*. Chicago, IL: University of Chicago Press, pp. 267–292.

1997. Culture and cognition. Annual Review of Sociology, pp. 263–287.

1983. State expansion and organizational fields. In R. H. Hall & R. E. Quinn, eds., *Organizational Theory and Public Policy*. Beverly Hills, CA: Sage, pp. 147–161.

1994. The challenge of community evolution. In J. A. C. Baum & J. V. Singh, eds., *Evolutionary Dynamics of Organizations*. New York: Oxford University Press., pp. 444–456.

DiMaggio, P., Nag, M., & Blei, D. 2013. Exploiting affinities between topic modeling and the sociological perspective on culture: Application to newspaper coverage of US government arts funding. *Poetics*, 41(6), pp. 570–606.

DiMaggio, P. J., & Powell, W. W. 1983. The iron cage revisited: Institutional isomorphism and collective rationality in organizational fields. *American Sociological Review*, 48(2), pp. 147–160.

1991. *The New Institutionalism in Organizational Analysis*. Chicago, IL: University of Chicago Press.

Dobbin, F. 1994. Cultural models of organization: The social construction of rational organizing principles. In D. Crane, ed., *The Sociology of Culture: Emerging Theoretical Perspectives* (pp. 117–141). Oxford, UK: Basil Blackwell.

Duguid, P. 2005. "The art of knowing": Social and tacit dimensions of knowledge and the limits of the community of practice. *The Information Society*, 21(2), pp. 109–118.

Duquenne, V. 1991. The core of finite lattices. *Discrete Mathematics*, 88(2–3), pp. 133–147.

Durand, R., & Calori, R. 2006. Sameness, otherness? Enriching organizational change theories with philosophical considerations on the same and the other. *Academy of Management Review*, 31(1), pp. 93–114.

Durand, R., & Kremp, P.-A. 2016. Classical deviation: Organizational and individual status as antecedents of conformity. *Academy of Management Journal*, 59(1), pp. 65–89.

Eisenhardt, K. M., & Schoonhoven, C. B. 1990. Organizational growth: Linking founding team, strategy, environment, and growth among US semiconductor ventures, 1978–1988. *Administrative Science Quarterly*, pp. 504–529.

Elsbach, K. D., & Glynn, M. A. 1996. Believing your own "PR": Embedding identification in strategic reputation. *Advances in Strategic Management*, 13, pp. 65–90.

Elsbach, K. D., & Kramer, R. M. 1996. Members' responses to organizational identity threats: Encountering and countering the Business Week rankings. Administrative Science Quarterly, 41(3), pp. 442–476.

Emirbayer, M. 1997. Manifesto for a relational sociology. *American Journal of Sociology*, 103(2), pp. 281–317.

Emirbayer, M., & Johnson, V. 2008. Bourdieu and organizational analysis. *Theory and Society*, 37(1), pp. 1–44.

Emirbayer, M., & Mische, A. 1998. What is agency? *American Journal of Sociology*, 103(4), pp. 962–1023.

Espeland, W. N., & Stevens, M. L. 1998. Commensuration as a social process. *Annual Review of Sociology*, 24(1), pp. 313–343.

Etzkowitz, H., Kemelgor, C., & Uzzi, B. 2000. *Athena Unbound: The Advancement of Women in Science and Technology*. Cambridge University Press.

Feldman, M. S., & March, J. G. 1981. Information in organizations as signal and symbol. Administrative Science Quarterly, 26(2), pp. 171–186.

Felin, T., & Zenger, T. R. 2009. Entrepreneurs as theorists: on the origins of collective beliefs and novel strategies. *Strategic Entrepreneurship Journal*, 3(2), pp. 127–146.

Fine, G. A. 1991. On the macrofoundations of microsociology. *Sociological Quarterly*, 32(2), pp. 161–177. Available at: http://dx.doi.org/10.1111/j.1533-8525.1991.tb00351.x.

Fisher, G., Kotha, S., & Lahiri, A. 2016. Changing with the times: An integrated view of identity, legitimacy and new venture life cycles. *Academy of Management Review*, 41(3), 383–409.

Fligstein, N., & McAdam, D. 2012. *A Theory of Fields*. Oxford University Press.

Foss, N. J., & Klein, P. G. 2012. *Organizing Entrepreneurial Judgment: A New Approach to the Firm*. Cambridge University Press.

Foss, N. J., Klein, P. G., & Bjørnskov, C. forthcoming. The context of entrepreneurial judgment: Organizations, markets and institutions. *Journal of Management Studies*.

Fourcade, M. 2009. Economists and Societies. Discipline and Profession in the United States, Britain, and France, 1890s to 1990s. Princeton, NJ: Princeton University Press.

Franzois, R. 1998. Narrative as data. Linguistic and statistical tools for the quantitative study of historical events. In M. van der Linden & L. Griffin, eds. *New Methods in Historical Sociology/Social History.* Cambridge, MA: Cambridge University Press., pp. 81–104.

Freeman, L. C., & White, D. R. 1993. Using Galois lattices to represent network data. Sociological Methodology, 23, pp. 127–146.

Friedland, R. 2009. The endless fields of Pierre Bourdieu. *Organization*, 16(6), pp. 887–917.

2018. Moving institutional logics forward: Emotion and meaningful material practice. *Organization Studies*, 39(4), pp. 515–542.

Friedland, R., & Mohr, J. 2004. *Matters of Culture: Cultural Sociology in Practice.* Cambridge University Press.

Furnari, S. 2014. Interstitial spaces: Microinteraction settings and the genesis of new practices between institutional fields. *Academy of Management Review*, 39(4), pp. 439–462.

Gabriel, Y. 2000. *Storytelling in Organizations: Facts, Fictions, and Fantasies: Facts, Fictions, and Fantasies.* Oxford University Press.

Gallo, C. 2016. *The Storyteller's Secret: From TED Speakers to Business Legends, Why Some Ideas Catch On and Others Don't.* New York, NY: St. Martin's Press.

Gamson, W. A. 1988. Political discourse and collective action. *International Social Movement Research*, 1(2), pp. 219–244.

1992. *Talking Politics.* New York, NY: Cambridge University Press.

Gamson, W. A., & Modigliani, A. 1989. Media discourse and public opinion on nuclear power: A constructionist approach. *American Journal of Sociology*, 95(1), pp. 1–37.

Gartner, W. B. 2007. Entrepreneurial narrative and a science of the imagination. *Journal of Business Venturing*, 22(5), pp. 613–627.

Gartner, W. B., Bird, B. J., & Starr, J. A. 1992. Acting as if: Differentiating entrepreneurial from organizational behavior. *Entrepreneurship Theory and Practice*, 16(3), pp. 13–31.

Gartner, W. B., & Carter, N. M. 2003. Entrepreneurial behavior and firm organizing processes. In Z. J. Acs & D. B. Audretsch, eds., *Handbook of Entrepreneurship Research: An Interdisciplinary Survey and Introduction.* Boston, MA: Springer US, pp. 195–221. Available at: https://doi.org/10.1007/0–387-24519–7_9.

Garud, R., Gehman, J., & Giuliani, A. P. 2014. Contextualizing entrepreneurial innovation: A narrative perspective. *Research Policy*, 43(7), pp. 1177–1188.

Garud, R., & Giuliani, A. P. 2013. A narrative perspective on entrepreneurial opportunities. *Academy of Management Review*, 38(1), pp. 157–160.

Garud, R., Schildt, H. A., & Lant, T. K. 2014. Entrepreneurial storytelling, future expectations, and the paradox of legitimacy. *Organization Science*, 25(5), pp. 1479–1492.

Forthcoming. Generative imitation, strategic distancing and optimal distinctiveness during the growth, decline and stabilization of Silicon Alley. Innovation: Organization and Management.

Gasse, Y., 1982. Elaborations on the psychology of the entrepreneur. Encyclopedia of Entrepreneurship, pp. 57–71.

Geertz, C. 1973. *The Interpretation of Cultures: Selected Essays*. New York, NY: Basic Books.

Gegenhuber, T., and Naderer, S. Forthcoming. When the petting zoo spawns into monsters: Open dialogue and a venture's legitimacy quest in crowdfunding. *Innovation: Organization and Management.*

Gehman, J., & Soublière, J.-F. 2017. Cultural entrepreneurship: from making culture to cultural making. *Innovation*, 19(1), pp. 61–73.

Gehman, J., Treviño, L. K., & Garud, R. (2013). Values work: a process study of the emergence and performance of organizational values practices. *Academy of Management Journal*, doi: 10.5465/amj.2010.0628, 56, 84–112.

Gerschenkron, A. 1962. *Economic Backwardness in Historical Perspective: A Book of Essays*. Belknap Press of Harvard University Press Cambridge, MA.

Giddens, A. 1981. *A Contemporary Critique of Historical Materialism*. University of California Press.

1979. *Central Problems in Social Theory: Action, Structure, and Contradiction in Social Analysis*. University of California Press.

Gilsing, V., et al. 2008. Network embeddedness and the exploration of novel technologies: Technological distance, betweenness centrality and density. *Research Policy*, 37(10), pp. 1717–1731.

Gioia, D. A., Schultz, M., & Corley, K. G. 2000. Organizational identity, image, and adaptive instability. *Academy of Management Review*, 25(1), pp. 63–81. Available at: http://search.ebscohost.com/login.aspx? direct=true&db=bth&AN=2791603&site=bsi-live.

Giorgi, S. 2017. The mind and heart of resonance: The role of cognition and emotions in frame effectiveness. *Journal of Management Studies*, 54(5), pp. 711–738.

Giorgi, S., Guider, M. E., & Bartunek, J. M. 2014. Productive resistance: A study of change, emotions, and identity in the context of the Apostolic Visitation of US women religious, 2008–2012. *Research in the Sociology of Organizations*, 41, pp. 259–300.

Giorgi, S., Lockwood, C., & Glynn, M. A. 2015. The many faces of culture: Making sense of 30 years of research on culture in organization studies. *The Academy of Management Annals*, 9(1), pp. 1–54.

Glaser, V. L. Forthcoming. Design performances: How organizations inscribe artifacts to change routines. Academy of Management Journal.

Glaser, V. L., Fiss, P. C., and Kennedy, M. T. 2016. Making snowflakes like stocks: Stretching, bending, and positioning to make financial market analogies work in online advertising. *Organization Science*, 27(4), 1029–1048.

Glynn, M. A. Forthcoming. *Living the Lifestyle: The Cultural Impact of Martha Stewart*. Stanford, CA: Stanford University Press.

2017. Theorizing the identity–institution relationship: Considering identity as antecedent to, consequence of, and mechanism for, processes of institutional change. In R. Greenwood et al., eds., *The SAGE Handbook of Organizational Institutionalism*.

2011. The "Martha" moment: Wading into others' worlds. In A. Carlsen & J. Dutton, eds., *Research Alive: Generative Moments for Doing Qualitative Research*, chapter 9, pp. 63–66. Copenhagen: Copenhagen Business School Press.

2008. Beyond constraint: How institutions enable identities. In K. Sahlin-Andersson et al., eds., *The Sage Handbook of Organizational Institutionalism*. London, UK: Sage Publications, pp. 413–430.

2000. When cymbals become symbols: Conflict over organizational identity within a symphony orchestra. Organization Science, 11(3, Special Issue: Cultural Industries: Learning from Evolving Organizational Practices), pp. 285–298.

Glynn, M. A., & Abzug, R. 2002. Institutionalizing identity: Symbolic isomorphism and organizational names. *Academy of Management Journal*, 45(1), pp. 267–280.

1998. Isomorphism and competitive differentiation in the organizational name game. *Advances in Strategic Management*, 1998, 15, pp. 105–128.

Glynn, M. A., & Dowd, T. 2008. Charisma (un)bound: Emotive leadership In Martha Stewart Living Magazine, 1990–2004. *Journal of Applied Behavioral Science*, 44, pp. 71–93.

Glynn, M. A., & Lounsbury, M. 2005. From the critics' corner: Logic blending, discursive change and authenticity in a cultural production system. *Journal of Management Studies*, 42(5), pp. 1031–1055.

Glynn, M. A., & Navis, C. 2013. Categories, identities, and cultural classification: Moving beyond a model of categorical constraint. *Journal of Management Studies*, 50(6), pp. 1124–1137.

Goffman, E. 1967. *Interaction Ritual: Essays on Face-to-Face Behavior.* Anchor Books.

1963. *Stigma; Notes on the Management of Spoiled Identity.* Englewood Cliffs, NJ: Prentice-Hall.

Golsorkhi, D., Leca, B., Lounsbury, M., & Ramirez, C. 2009. Analysing, accounting for and unmasking domination: On our role as scholars of practice, practitioners of social science and public intellectuals. *Organization*, 16, pp. 779–797.

Graddy, E., & Wang, L. 2009. Community foundation development and social capital. *Nonprofit and Voluntary Sector Quarterly*, 38(3), pp. 392–412.

Granovetter, M. 1985. Economic action and social structure: The problem of embeddedness.*American Journal of Sociology*, 91(3), pp. 481–510. Available at: www.jstor.org/stable/2780199.

Granqvist, N., Grodal, S., & Woolley, J. L. 2013. Hedging your bets: Explaining executives' market labeling strategies in nanotechnology. *Organization Science*, 24(2), pp. 395–413.

Greenwood, R., et al. 2017. *The SAGE Handbook of Organizational Institutionalism.* SAGE.

Greenwood, R., & Hinings, C. R. 1996. Understanding radical organizational change: Bringing together the old and the new institutionalism. *The Academy of Management Review*, 21(4), pp. 1022–1054. Available at: www.jstor.org/stable/259163.

Greenwood, R., Raynard, M., Kodeih, F., Micelotta, E., & Lounsbury, M. 2011. Institutional complexity and organizational responses. *Academy of Management Annals*, 5, 317–371.

Griliches, Z. 1992. Introduction to "output measurement in the service sectors." In *Output Measurement in the Service Sectors*. University of Chicago Press, pp. 1–22.

Grimes, M. G. 2018. The pivot: How founders respond to feedback through idea and identity work. *Academy of Management Journal*, 61, pp. 1692–1717.

Griswold, W. 1994. *Cultures and Societies in a Changing World*, Thousand Oaks, CA: Sage Publications.

Haans, R. F. J. Forthcoming. What's the value of being different when everyone is? The effects of distinctiveness on performance in homogeneous versus heterogeneous categories. Strategic Management Journal.

Hall, B. H., Jaffe, A. B., & Trajtenberg, M. 2001. *The NBER Patent Citation Data File: Lessons, Insights and Methodological Tools*. National Bureau of Economic Research.

Hannigan, T. 2015. Close encounters of the conceptual kind: Disambiguating social structure from text. *Big Data & Society*, 2(2), pp. 1–6.

Hardy, C., & Maguire, S. 2010. Discourse, field-configuring events, and change in organizations and institutional fields: Narratives of DDT and the Stockholm Convention. *Academy of Management Journal*, 53(6), pp. 1365–1392.

2008. Institutional entrepreneurship. The Sage Handbook of Organizational Institutionalism, pp. 198–217.

Harmon, D. Forthcoming. When the Fed speaks: Arguments, emotions, and the microfoundations of institutions. Administrative Science Quarterly.

Harmon, D., Green, S., & Goodnight, G. 2015. A model of rhetorical legitimation: The structure of communication and cognition underlying institutional maintenance and change. *Academy of Management Review*, 40(1), pp. 76–95.

Hargadon, A., & Sutton, R. I. 1997. Technology brokering and innovation in a product development firm. *Administrative Science Quarterly*, pp. 716–749.

Hays, S. 2000. Constructing the centrality of culture and deconstructing sociology. *Contemporary Sociology*, 29, pp. 594–602.

Hayward, M. L. A., Rindova, V. P., & Pollock, T. G. 2004. Believing One's Own Press: The Causes and Consequences of. *Strategic Management Journal*, 25, pp. 637–653. Available at: www.interscience.wiley.com.

Helfat, C. E., et al. 2007. *Dynamic Capabilities: Understanding Strategic Change in Organizations*. Wiley-Blackwell; 1st edition (January 16, 2007).

Helfat, C. E., & Peteraf, M. A. 2009. Understanding dynamic capabilities: Progress along a developmental path. *Strategic Organization*, 7(1), pp. 91–102.

Hirsch, P. M. 2000. Cultural industries revisited. *Organization Science*, 11(3), pp. 356–361.

1972. Processing fads and fashions: An organization-set analysis of cultural industry systems. *American Journal of Sociology*, 77(4), pp. 639–659.

1997. Sociology without social structure: New institutional theory meets brave new world. *American Journal of Sociology*, 102(6), pp. 1702–1723.

Hirsch, P. M., & Lounsbury, M. 1997. Putting the organization back into organization theory: Action, change, and the "new" institutionalism. *Journal of Management Inquiry*, 6(1), pp. 79–88.

Hitt, M.A., et al. 2002. Strategic entrepreneurship: Integrating entrepreneurial and strategic management perspectives. *Strategic Entrepreneurship: Creating a New Mindset*, pp. 1–16.

Hjorth, D., & Steyaert, C. (Eds.) 2004. *Narrative and discursive approaches in entrepreneurship: A second movements in entrepreneurship book*. Northampton, MA: Edward Elgar Publishing.

Hofstede, G. 1980. *Culture's Consequences : International Differences in Work-Related Values*. Beverly Hills, CA: Sage Publications.

Höllerer, M. A., Daudigeos, T., & Jancsary, D. (Eds.). 2018. Multimodality, meaning, and institutions. *Research in the Sociology of Organizations*, 54(A-B). Bingley, UK: Emerald Group Publishing.

Hoselitz, B. F. 1963. Entrepreneurship and traditional elites. *Explorations in Economic History*, 1(1), p. 36.

Hughes, K. D., & Jennings, J. E. 2015. Women's entrepreneurship. In R. Griffen, ed. *Oxford Bibliographies in Management*. New York: Oxford University Press.

Ibarra, H., & Barbulescu, R. 2010. Identity as narrative: Prevalence, effectiveness, and consequences of narrative identity work in macro work role transitions. *Academy of Management Review*, 35(1), pp. 135–154.

Ireland, R. D., Hitt, M. A., & Sirmon, D. G. 2003. A model of strategic entrepreneurship: The construct and its dimensions. *Journal of Management*, 29(6), pp. 963–989.

Jaffe, A. B. 1986. *Technological Opportunity and Spillovers of R&D: Evidence from Firms' Patents, Profits and Market Value*. National Bureau of Economic Research Cambridge, MA, USA.

Jaffe, A. B., & Trajtenberg, M. 2002. *Patents, Citations, and Innovations: A Window on the Knowledge Economy*. Massachusetts Institute of Technology Press.

Jennings, J. E., et al. 2015. Emotional arousal and entrepreneurial outcomes: Combining qualitative methods to elaborate theory. *Journal of Business Venturing*, 30(1), pp. 113–130.

Jennings, J. E., & Brush, C. G. 2013. Research on women entrepreneurs: challenges to (and from) the broader entrepreneurship literature? *Academy of Management Annals*, 7(1), pp. 663–715.

Johnson, V. 2007. What is organizational imprinting? Cultural entrepreneurship in the founding of the Paris Opera. *American Journal of Sociology*, 113(1), pp. 97–127.

Jones, C., Lorenzen, M., & Sapsed, J. 2015. *The Oxford Handbook of Creative Industries*, Oxford Handbooks.

Kaplan, S. 2015. Mixing qualitative and quantitative research methods. In K. Elsbach & R. Kramer, eds. *Handbook of Qualitative Organizational Research: Innovative Pathways and Methods*. Taylor & Francis, pp. 423–433.

Kaplan, S., & Vakili, K. 2015. The double-edged sword of recombination in breakthrough innovation. *Strategic Management Journal*, 36(10), pp. 1435–1457.

Kazanjian, R. K., Drazin, R., & Glynn, M. A. 2002. Implementing strategies for corporate entrepreneurship: A knowledge-based perspective. *Strategic Entrepreneurship: Creating a New Mindset*, pp. 173–199.

Kennedy M. T. 2005. Behind the one-way mirror: Refraction in the construction of product market categories. *POETICS*, 33, pp. 201–226.

Kennedy, M. T., & Fiss, P. C. 2013. An ontological turn in categories research: From standards of legitimacy to evidence of actuality. *Journal of Management Studies*, 50(6), pp. 1138–1154.

Kenney, M. 2000. *Understanding Silicon Valley: The Anatomy of an Entrepreneurial Region*. Stanford: Stanford University Press.

Khaire, M. 2017. *Culture and Commerce: The Value of Entrepreneurship in Creative Industries*. Palo Alto, CA: Stanford University Press.

Kirzner, I. M. 1973. *Competition and Entrepreneurship*. University of Chicago Press.

1979. *Perception, Opportunity, and Profit*. Chicago, IL: University of Chicago Press.

Knight, F. H. 1921. *Risk, Uncertainty and Profit*. Houghton Mifflin Company.

Kolb, B. 2015. *Entrepreneurship for the Creative and Cultural Industries*. Routledge.

Korsgaard, S., et al. 2016. A tale of two Kirzners: Time, uncertainty, and the "nature" of opportunities. *Entrepreneurship Theory and Practice*, 40(4), pp. 867–889. Available at: http://dx.doi.org/10.1111/etap.12151.

Kraatz, M. S., & Block, E. S. 2008. Organizational implications of institutional pluralism. The SAGE Handbook of Organizational Institutionalism, 840.

Kraatz, M. S., & Zajac, E. J. 1996. Exploring the limits of the new institutionalism: The causes and consequences of illegitimate organizational change. American Sociological Review, 61(5) pp. 812–836.

Kroto, H. W., et al. 1985. C60: Buckminsterfullerene. *Nature*, 318(6042), pp. 162–163.

Kubal, T. J. 1998. The presentation of political self. *The Sociological Quarterly*, 39(4), pp. 539–554.

Kuhn, T. 1970. *The Structure of Scientific Revolutions*. Second Ed., Chicago: University of Chicago Press.

Lakatos, I. 1978. Science and pseudoscience. *Philosophical Papers*, 1, pp. 1–7.

Lamont, M., & Lareau, A. 1988. Cultural capital: Allusions, gaps and glissandos in recent theoretical developments. *Sociological Theory*, 6(2), pp. 153–168. Available at: www.jstor.org/stable/202113.

Lamont, M., & Molnár, V. 2002. The study of boundaries across the social sciences. *Annual Review of Sociology*, 28, pp. 167–195.

Lampel, J., & Meyer, A. D. 2008. Guest editors' introduction: Field-configuring events as structuring mechanisms: How conferences, ceremonies, and trade shows constitute new technologies, industries, and markets. *Journal of Management Studies*, 45(6), pp. 1025–1035.

Lawrence, T. B., & Suddaby, R. 2006. Institutions and institutional work. In S. R. Clegg et al., eds., *The Sage Handbook of Organization Studies*. Thousand Oaks, CA: Sage Publications Limited, pp. 215–254.

Leadbeater, C., & Oakley, K. 1999. *The Independents: Britain's New Cultural Entrepreneurs*, Demos.

Lee, B. H., Hiatt, S. R., & Lounsbury, M. 2017. Market mediators and the trade-offs of legitimacy seeking behaviors in a nascent category. *Organization Science*, 28: pp. 447–470.

Lieber, C. 2003. Harvard's Charles M. Lieber: An inside line on nanowires. *Science Watch*, 14, pp. 1–5.

Light, I. H., & Rosenstein, C. N. 1995. *Race, Ethnicity, and Entrepreneurship in Urban America*. Transaction Publishers.

Lingo, E. L., & O'Mahony, S. 2010. Nexus Work: Brokerage on Creative Projects. *Administrative Science Quarterly*, 55(1), pp. 47–81. Available at: http://search.ebscohost.com/login.aspx?direct=true&db=bth&AN=50051945&site=bsi-live.

Lippert, B. 1995. Our Martha, ourselves. *New York Magazine*. Available at: http://nymag.com/news/media/48253/.

Lizardo, O. 2014. Omnivorousness as the bridging of cultural holes: A measurement strategy. *Theory and Society*, 43(3–4), pp.395–419.

Lounsbury, M. 2007. A tale of two cities: Competing logics and practice variation in the professionalizing of mutual funds. *Academy of Management Journal*, 50(2), pp. 289–307.

    1998. Collective entrepreneurship: The mobilization of college and university recycling coordinators. *Journal of Organizational Change Management*, 11, pp. 50–69.

Lounsbury, M., & Beckman, C. M. 2015. Celebrating organization theory. *Journal of Management Studies*, 52(2), pp. 288–308.

Lounsbury, M., & Boxenbaum, E. 2013. Institutional logics in action. In *Institutional Logics in Action, Part A*. Emerald Group Publishing Limited, pp. 3–22.

Lounsbury, M., Cornelissen, J., Granqvist, N., & Grodal, S. Forthcoming. Culture, innovation and entrepreneurship. Innovation: Organization and Management.

Lounsbury, M., & Crumley, E. T. 2007. New practice creation: An institutional perspective on innovation. *Organization Studies*, 28(7), pp. 993–1012.

Lounsbury, M., & Glynn, M. A. 2001. Cultural entrepreneurship: Stories, legitimacy, and the acquisition of resources. *Strategic Management Journal*, 22(6), p. 545.

Lounsbury, M., & Rao, H. 2004. Sources of durability and change in market classifications: A study of the reconstitution of product categories in the American mutual fund industry, 1944–1985. *Social Forces*, 82(3), pp. 969–999.

Lounsbury, M., & Ventresca, M. 2003. The new structuralism in organizational theory. *Organization*, 10(3), pp. 457–480.

Lounsbury, M., Ventresca, M., & Hirsch, P. M. 2003. Social movements, field frames and industry emergence: a cultural–political perspective on US recycling. *Socio-Economic Review*, 1(1), pp. 71–104.

Lounsbury, M., Wry, T., & Devereaux Jennings, P. 2010. The politics of neglect: Path selection and development in nanotechnology innovation. In *Spanning Boundaries and Disciplines: University Technology Commercialization in the Idea Age*. Emerald Group Publishing Limited, pp. 27–58.

Lux Venture Capital. 2006 "The nanotech report: Investment overview and market research for nanotechnology, 4th Ed."

Mantere, S., et al. 2013. Narrative attributions of entrepreneurial failure. *Journal of Business Venturing*, 28(4), pp. 459–473.

Markusen, A. 2013. Fuzzy concepts, proxy data: why indicators would not track creative placemaking success. *International Journal of Urban Sciences*, 17(3), pp. 291–303.

Marquis, C., Lounsbury, M., & Greenwood, R. 2011. Community as an institutional order and type of organizing. *Research in the Sociology of Organizations*, 33, ix–xxvii.

Martens, M. L., Jennings, J. E., & Jennings, P. D. 2007. Do the stories they tell get them the money they need? The role of entrepreneurial narratives in resource acquisition. *The Academy of Management Journal*, 50(5), pp. 1107–1132.

Martin, J. 1992. *Cultures in Organizations: Three Perspectives*. Oxford, UK: Oxford University Press.

Martin, J. L. 2003. What is field theory? *American Journal of Sociology*, 109, pp. 1–49.

Martinelli, A. 1994. Entrepreneurship and management. *The Handbook of Economic Sociology*, pp. 476–503.

Massa, F. G., Helms, W. S., Voronov, M., & Wang, L. (2017). Emotions uncorked: Inspiring evangelism for the emerging practice of cool-climate winemaking in Ontario. *Academy of Management Journal*, doi: 10.5465/amj.2014.0092, 60, 461–499.

McDonald, R., & Eisenhardt, K. Forthcoming. Parallel play: Startups, nascent markets, and the search for a viable business model. *Administrative Science Quarterly*.

McDonald, R., & Gao, C. 2017 (July–August). Entrepreneurship: Every pivot needs a story. *Harvard Business Review*, 95: 24.

McMullen, J. S., Plummer, L. A., & Acs, Z. J. 2007. What is an entrepreneurial opportunity? *Small Business Economics*, 28(4), pp. 273–283.

McMullen, J. S., & Shepherd, D. A. 2006. Entrepreneurial action and the role of uncertainty in the theory of the entrepreneur. *Academy of Management Review*, 31(1), pp. 132–152.

McPherson, C. M., & Sauder, M. 2013. Logics in action: Managing institutional complexity in a drug court. *Administrative Science Quarterly*, 58(2), pp. 165–196.

Mead, G. H. 1932. *The Philosophy of the Present* 1980 ed., University of Chicago Press. Available at: https://books.google.com/books?id=nLiVDAEACAAJ.

Meyer, J. W., et al. 1997. World society and the nation-state. *American Journal of Sociology*, 103(1), pp. 144–181.

Meyer, J. W., Boli, J., & Thomas, G. M. 1987. Ontology and rationalization in the western cultural account. *Institutional Structure: Constituting State, Society, and the Individual*, pp. 12–37.

Meyer, J. W., & Rowan, B. 1977. Institutionalized organizations: Formal structure as myth and ceremony. *American Journal of Sociology*, 83(2), pp. 340–363.

Meyer, J. W., & Scott, W. R. 1983. Centralization and the legitimacy problems of local government. In *Organizational Environments: Ritual and Rationality*. Beverly Hills, CA: Sage, pp. 199–215.

Meyer, R. E., & Höllerer, M. A. 2010. Meaning structures in a contested issue field: A topographic map of shareholder value in Austria. *Academy of Management Journal*, 53(6), pp. 1241–1262.

Micelotta, E., Lounsbury, M., & Greenwood, R. 2017. Pathways of institutional change: An integrative review and research agenda. *Journal of Management*, 43: pp. 1885–1910

Milkie, M. A., & Denny, K. E. 2014. Changes in the cultural model of father involvement: Descriptions of benefits to fathers, children, and mothers in Parents' Magazine, 1926–2006. *Journal of Family Issues*, 35(2), pp. 223–253.

Mische, A. 2014. Measuring futures in action: Projective grammars in the Rio+20 debates. *Theory and Society*, 43(3–4), pp. 437–464.

2009. Projects and possibilities: Researching futures in action. In *Sociological Forum*. Wiley Online Library, pp. 694–704.

Mische, A., & Pattison, P. 2000. Composing a civic arena: Publics, projects, and social settings. *Poetics*, 27(2–3), pp. 163–194.

MIT Technology Review. March 1, 2001. Wires of Wonder. www.technologyreview.com/s/400912/wires-of-wonder/ (Accessed on October 27, 2018).

Mody, C. 2011. *Instrumental Community: Probe Microscopy and the Path to Nanotechnology*. MIT Press.

Mohr, J. W. 1998. Measuring meaning structures. *Annual Review of Sociology*, 24, pp. 345–370.

Mohr, J. W., & Ghaziani, A. 2014. Problems and prospects of measurement in the study of culture. *Theory and Society*, 43(3–4), pp. 225–246.

Mohr, J. W., & Guerra-Pearson, F. 2010. The duality of niche and form: The differentiation of institutional space in New York City, 1888–1917. In *Categories in Markets: Origins and Evolution*. Emerald Group Publishing Limited, pp. 321–368.

Mohr, J. W., & White, H. C. 2008. How to model an institution. *Theory and Society*, 37(5), pp. 485–512.

Navis, C., & Glynn, M. A. 2010. How new market categories emerge: Temporal dynamics of legitimacy, identity, and entrepreneurship in satellite radio, 1990–2005. *Administrative Science Quarterly*, 55(3), pp. 439–471.

2011. Legitimate distinctiveness and the entrepreneurial identity: Influence on investor judgments of new venture plausibility. *Academy of Management Review*, 36(3), pp. 479–499.

Nicholls, A. 2010. The legitimacy of social entrepreneurship: reflexive isomorphism in a pre-paradigmatic field. *Entrepreneurship Theory and Practice*, 34(4), pp. 611–633.

Obstfeld, D. 2005. Social networks, the tertius iungens orientation, and involvement in innovation. *Administrative Science Quarterly*, 50(1), pp. 100–130. Available at: http://search.ebscohost.com/login.aspx?direct=true&db=bth&AN=17521509&site=bsi-live.

Ocasio, W., Mauskapf, M., & Steele, C. W. J. 2016. History, society, and institutions: The role of collective memory in the emergence and evolution of societal logics. *Academy of Management Review*, 41(4): 676–699.

Olson, Mancur. 1996. Distinguished lecture on economics in government: Big bills left on the sidewalk: Why some nations are rich, and others poor. *The Journal of Economic Perspectives*, 10, pp. 3–24

Pachucki, M. A., & Breiger, R. L. 2010. Cultural holes: Beyond relationality in social networks and culture. *Annual Review of Sociology*, 36, pp. 205–224.

Padgett, J. F., & Powell, W. W. 2012. *The Emergence of Organizations and Markets*. Princeton University Press.

Pahnke, E. C., Katila, R., & Eisenhardt, K. M. 2015. Who takes you to the dance? How partners' institutional logics influence innovation in young firms. *Administrative Science Quarterly*. 60(4): pp. 596–633.

Parsons, T. 1937. *The Structure of Social Action*. New York: McGraw Hill.

Pedersen, J. S., & Dobbin, F. 2006. In search of identity and legitimation: Bridging organizational culture and neoinstitutionalism. *American Behavioral Scientist*, 49(7), pp. 897–907.

Peterson, R. A. 1978. The production of cultural change: The case of contemporary country music. *Social Research*, 45(2), pp. 292–314. Available at: www.jstor.org/stable/40970334.

1977. *The Production of Culture*. Beverly Hills, CA: Sage.

Pfeffer, J. 1981. *Power in Organizations*. Marshfield, MA: Pitman.

Philippe, D., & Durand, R. 2011. The impact of norm-conforming behaviors on firm reputation. *Strategic Management Journal*, 32(9), pp. 969–993.

Phillips, N., & Hardy, C. 1997. Managing multiple identities: Discourse, legitimacy and resources in the UK refugee system. *Organization*, 4(2), pp. 159–185. Available at: https://doi.org/10.1177/135050849742002.

Pinchot III, G. 1985. *Intrapreneuring: Why You Don't Have to Leave the Corporation to Become an Entrepreneur*. New York: Harper & Row.

Podolny, J. M., & Stuart, T. E. 1995. A role-based ecology of technological change. *American Journal of Sociology*, 100(5), pp. 1224–1260.

Poletta, F. 2006. *It Was Like a Fever: Storytelling in Protest and Politics*. University of Chicago Press.

Porter, M. E. 1996. What is strategy? *Harvard Business Review*, 74(6), pp. 61–78.

Portes, A. 1995. *The Economic Sociology of Immigration: Essays on Networks, Ethnicity, and Entrepreneurship*. Russell Sage Foundation.

Powell, W. W., & Colyvas, J. A. 2008. Microfoundations of institutional theory. In K. Sahlin-Andersson et al., eds., *The Sage Handbook of Organizational Institutionalism*. London, UK: Sage Publications, p. 298.

Rao, H. 1994. The social construction of reputation: Certification contests, legitimation, and the survival of organizations in the American automobile industry: 1895–1912. *Strategic Management Journal*, 15(S1), pp. 29–44.

Rao, H., Monin, P., & Durand, R. 2005. Border crossing: Bricolage and the erosion of categorical boundaries in French gastronomy. *American Sociological Review*, 70(6), pp. 968–991.

2003. Institutional change in Toque Ville: Nouvelle cuisine as an identity movement in French gastronomy. *American Journal of Sociology*, 108(4), pp. 795–843.

Rao, H., Morrill, C., & Zald, M. N. 2000. Power plays: How social movements and collective action create new organizational forms. *Research in Organizational Behavior*, 22, pp. 237–281.

Ravasi, D., & Rindova, V. 2008. Symbolic value creation. *Handbook of New Approaches to Organization*, pp. 270–284.

Reay, T., & Hinings, C. R. 2009. Managing the rivalry of competing institutional logics. *Organization Studies*, 30, pp. 629–652.

Ricoeur, P. 1991. Narrative identity. *Philosophy Today*, pp. 73–81.

Rindova, V., & Fombrun, C. 2001. The growth of the specialty coffee niche in the U.S. coffee industry. In K. Bird-Schoonhoven & E. Romanelli, eds., *The Entrepreneurship Dynamic*. Stanford University Press.

Rindova, V. P., Petkova, A. P., & Kotha, S. 2007. Standing out: how new firms in emerging markets build reputation. *Strategic Organization*, 5(1), pp. 31–70.

Rindova, V. P., Pollock, T. G., & Hayward, M. L. A. 2006. Celebrity firms: The social construction of market popularity. *Academy of Management Review*, 31(1), pp. 50–71.

Rosenkopf, L., & Nerkar, A. 2001. Beyond local search: boundary-spanning, exploration, and impact in the optical disk industry. *Strategic Management Journal*, 22(4), pp. 287–306.

Ruef, M. 1999. The dynamics of organizational forms: Creating market actors in the healthcare field, 1966–94. *Social Forces*, 77(4), pp. 1405–1434.

2000. The emergence of organizational forms: A community ecology approach. *American Journal of Sociology*, 106(3), pp. 658–714. Available at: www.jstor.org/stable/10.1086/318963.

2010. *The Entrepreneurial Group: Social Identities, Relations, and Collective Action*. Princeton, NJ: Princeton University Press.

Ruef, M., Aldrich, H. E., & Carter, N. M. 2003. The structure of founding teams: Homophily, strong ties, and isolation among U.S. entrepreneurs. *American Sociological Review*, 68(2), pp. 195–222. Available at: http://proxy.bc.edu/login?url=https://search.proquest.com/docview/218822087?accountid=9673.

Ruef, M., & Lounsbury, M. 2007. Introduction: The sociology of entrepreneurship. In *The Sociology of Entrepreneurship*. Emerald Group Publishing Limited, pp. 1–29.

Ruef, M., & Scott, W. R. 1998. A multidimensional model of organizational legitimacy: Hospital survival in changing institutional environments. *Administrative Science Quarterly*, 43(4), pp. 877–904. Available at: www.jstor.org/stable/2393619.

Sanders, M. 2007. Scientific paradigms, entrepreneurial opportunities and cycles in economic growth. *Small Business Economics*, 28(4), pp. 339–354.

Santos, F. M., & Eisenhardt, K. M. 2009. Constructing markets and shaping boundaries: Entrepreneurial power in nascent fields. *Academy of Management Journal*, 52(4), pp. 643–671.

Sarasvathy, S. D. 2008. *Effectuation: Elements of Entrepreneurial Expertise*. New Horizon, Edward Elgar Publishing.

Sartre, J.-P. 2000 (1938). *Nausea*. New York: Penguin Books.

Schatzki, T. R. 2003. *The Site of the Social: A Philosophical Account of the Constitution of Social Life and Change*. University Park, PA: Penn State University Press.

Schatzki, T. R., Knorr-Cetina, K., & Savigny, E. v. (Eds.). 2001. *The Practice Turn in Contemporary Theory*. London: Routledge.

Schneiberg, M., & Clemens, E. S. 2006. The typical tools for the job: Research strategies in institutional analysis. *Sociological Theory*, 24(3), pp. 195–227. Available at: www.jstor.org/stable/25046721.

Schneiberg, M., & Lounsbury, M. 2017. Social movements and the dynamics of institutions and organizations. In R. Greenwood et al., eds., *Sage Handbook of Organizational Institutionalism*. London: Sage, pp. 297–327.

Schumpeter, J. A. 1934. *The Theory of Economic Development: An Inquiry Into Profits, Capital, Credit, Interest, and the Business Cycle*. Transaction Publishers.

Schutz, A. 1951. Choosing among projects of action. *Philosophy and Phenomenological Research*, 12, pp. 161–184.

   1967. *The Phenomenology of the Social World*, Evanston, IL: Northwestern University Press.

Scott, M. B., & Lyman, S. M. 1968. Accounts. *American Sociological Review*, 33, pp. 46–62.

Scott, P. 1995. *The Meanings of Mass Higher Education*. McGraw-Hill Education (UK).

Scott, W. R. 2014. *Institutions and Organizations: Ideas and Interests*, 4th ed. Thousand Oaks, CA: Sage Publications.

Seidel, M.-D. L., & Greve, H. R. 2017. Emergence: How novelty, growth, and formation shape organizations and their ecosystems. In *Emergence*. Emerald Publishing Limited, pp. 1–27.

Seidel, V. P., & O'Mahony, S. 2014. Managing the repertoire: Stories, metaphors, prototypes, and concept coherence in product innovation. *Organization Science*, 25(3), pp. 691–712.

Seidel, V. P., Hannigan, T. R., & Phillips, N. Forthcoming. Rumor communities, social media, and forthcoming innovations: The shaping of technological frames in product market evolution. *Academy of Management Review.*

Sewell, W. H. 1992. A theory of structure: Duality, agency, and transformation. *American Journal of Sociology,* 98(1), pp. 1–29.

Shackle, G. L. S. 1979. *Imagination and the Nature of Choice.* Columbia University Press.

Shane, S. A. 2003. *A General Theory of Entrepreneurship: The Individual-Opportunity Nexus.* Edward Elgar Publishing.

Shane, S., & Venkataraman, S. 2000. The promise of entrepreneurship as a field of research. *Academy of Management Review,* 25(1), pp. 217–226.

Shapero, A., & Sokol, L. 1982. The social dimensions of entrepreneurship. *Encyclopedia of Entrepreneurship.* Englewood Cliffs, NJ: Prentice-Hall, pp. 72–90.

Shepherd, D. A., & Patzelt, H. 2017. *Trailblazing in Entrepreneurship: Creating New Paths for Understanding the Field.* Springer.

Shepherd, D. A., Patzelt, H., & Wolfe, M., 2011. Moving forward from project failure: Negative emotions, affective commitment, and learning from the experience. *Academy of Management Journal,* 54(6), pp. 1229–1259.

Shiller, R. J. 2017. Narrative economics. *The American Economic Review,* 107(4), pp. 967–1004.

Shrum, W. 1991. Critics and publics: Cultural mediation in highbrow and popular performing arts. *American Journal of Sociology,* 97(2), pp. 347–375.

Simmel, G. 1990. *The Philosophy of Money.* London: Routledge.

Simmel, G., & Wolff, K. H. 1950. *The Sociology of Georg Simmel.* Simon and Schuster.

Sine, W. D., David, R. J., & Mitsuhashi, H. 2007. From plan to plant: Effects of certification on operational start-up in the emergent independent power sector. *Organization Science,* 18(4), pp. 578–594.

Sine, W. D., & Lee, B. H. 2009. Tilting at windmills? The environmental movement and the emergence of the U.S. wind energy sector. Administrative Science Quarterly, 54(1), pp. 123–155. Available at: www.jstor.org/stable/27749308.

Slade Shantz, A., Kistruck, G., & Zietsma, C. 2018. The opportunity not taken: The occupational identity of entrepreneurs in contexts of poverty. *Journal of Business Venturing,* doi: 10.1016/j.jbusvent.2018.02.003.

Smets, M., Aristidou, A., & Whittington, R. 2017. Towards a practice-driven institutionalism. In R. Greenwood, C. Oliver, T. B. Lawrence, & R.

Meyer, eds., The Sage Handbook of Organizational Institutionalism, 2nd ed. London: Sage, pp. 384–411.

Smircich, L. 1983. Concepts of culture and organizational analysis. *Administrative Science Quarterly*, 28(3), pp. 339–358. Available at: http://search.ebscohost.com/login.aspx?direct=true&db=bth&AN=3980 622&site=bsi-live.

Snow, D. A., et al. 1986. Frame alignment processes, micromobilization, and movement participation. *American Sociological Review*, 51(4), pp. 464–481.

Snow, D. A., & Benford, R. D. 1988. Ideology, frame resonance, and participant mobilization. *International Social Movement Research*, 1(1), pp. 197–217.

1992. Master frames and cycles of protest. *Frontiers in Social Movement Theory*, 133, p. 155.

de Solla Price, D. 1965. *Little Science, Big Science*. New York: Columbia University Press.

Somers, M. R. 1993. Citizenship and the place of the public sphere: law, community, and political culture in the transition to democracy. *American Sociological Review*, pp. 587–620.

Sorin, G. S., & Sessions, L. A. 2015. *Case Studies in Cultural Entrepreneurship How to Create Relevant and Sustainable Institutions · American Association for State and Local History*. Lanham, MD: Rowman & Littlefield Publishing Co.

Spillman, L. 2002. Introduction: Culture and cultural sociology. *Cultural Sociology*, pp. 1–15.

Stark, R. 2007. *Sociology*. Wadsworth.

Stewart, A. 1989. *Team Entrepreneurship*, Newbury Park, CA: Sage.

Stewart, M. 1997. (April), Letter. *Martha Stewart Living*, p. 12.

Stokes, R., & Hewitt, J. P. 1976. Aligning actions. *American Sociological Review*, 41: 838–849.

Strang, D., & Meyer, J. W. 1993. Institutional conditions for diffusion. *Theory and Society*, 22(4), pp. 487–511.

Strang, D., & Soule, S. A. 1998. Diffusion in organizations and social movements: From hybrid corn to poison pills. *Annual Review of Sociology*, 24(1), pp. 265–290.

Stryker, R. 1994. Rules, resources, and legitimacy processes: Some implications for social conflict, order, and change. *American Journal of Sociology*, 99(4), pp. 847–910.

Suchman, M. C. 1995. Managing legitimacy: Strategic and institutional approaches. *Academy of Management Review*, 20(3), pp. 571–610.

Swedberg, R. 1991. Major traditions of economic sociology. Annual Review of Sociology, 17(1), pp. 251–276. Available at: https://doi.org/10.1146/annurev.so.17.080191.001343.

Swidler, A. 1986. Culture in action: Symbols and strategies. *American Sociological Review*, 51(2), pp. 273–286.

2001. What anchors cultural practices. In K. Knorr-Cetina, T. R. Schatzki, & E. von Savigny, eds., *The Practice Turn in Contemporary Theory.* New York, NY: Routledge, pp. 74–92.

Tavory, I., & Eliasoph, N. 2013. Coordinating futures: toward a theory of anticipation. *American Journal of Sociology*, 118(4), pp. 908–942.

Thornton, P. H. 1999. The sociology of entrepreneurship. *Annual Review of Sociology*, 25(1), pp. 19–46.

Thornton, P. H., & Flynn, K. H. 2003. Networks, geographies, and entrepreneurship. In Z. J. Acs & D. B. Audretsch, eds., *The Handbook of Entrepreneurship.* Kluwer Academic Publishers.

Thornton, P. H., Ocasio, W., & Lounsbury, M. 2012. *The Institutional Logics Perspective: A New Approach to Culture, Structure, and Process.* Oxford, UK: Oxford University Press.

Tolbert, P. S., & Zucker, L. G. 1983. Institutional sources of change in the formal structure of organizations: The diffusion of civil service reform, 1880–1935. *Administrative Science Quarterly*, pp. 22–39.

Toubiana, M., & Zietsma, C. 2017. The message is on the wall: Emotions, social media, and the dynamics of institutional complexity. *Academy of Management Journal*, 60, 922–953.

Tracey, P., Dalpaiz, E., & Phillips, N. 2018. Fish out of water: Translation, legitimation, and new venture creation. *Academy of Management Journal*, 61, pp. 1627–1666.

Überbacher, F. 2014. Legitimation of new ventures: A review and research programme. *Journal of Management Studies*, 51(4), pp. 667–698.

Überbacher, F., Jacobs, C. D., & Cornelissen, J. P. 2015. How entrepreneurs become skilled cultural operators. *Organization Studies*, 36(7), pp. 925–951.

Vaara, E., Sonenshein, S., & Boje, D., 2016. Narratives as sources of stability and change in organizations: Approaches and directions for future research. *The Academy of Management Annals*, 10(1), pp. 495–560.

van Werven, R., Bouwmeester, O., & Cornelissen, J. P. 2015. The power of arguments: How entrepreneurs convince stakeholders of the legitimate distinctiveness of their ventures. *Journal of Business Venturing*, 30(4), pp. 616–631.

Venkataraman, S. 2000. Note the promise of entrepreneurship as a field of research. University of Maryland. Review Literature and Arts of the Americas, 25(1), pp. 217–226. Available at: www.jstor.org/stable/259388.
1997. The distinctive domain of entrepreneurship research. *Advances in Entrepreneurship, Firm Emergence and Growth*, 3(1), pp. 119–138.

Voronov, M. 2014. Toward a toolkit for emotionalizing institutional theory. *Research on Emotion in Organizations*, 10, pp. 167–196.

Voronov, M., De Clercq, D., & Hinings, C. R. 2013. Conformity and distinctiveness in a global institutional framework: The legitimation of Ontario fine wine. *Journal of Management Studies*, 50 (4), pp. 607–645.

Voronov, M., & Vince, R. 2012. Integrating emotions into the analysis of institutional work. *Academy of Management Review*, 37 (1): pp. 58–81

Voronov, M., & Weber, K. 2017. Emotional competence, institutional ethos and the heart of institutions. *Academy of Management Review*, 42 (1): pp. 556–560.

Voss, K., 1998. Claim making and the framing of defeats: The interpretation of losses by American and British Labor Activists, 1886–1895. *Challenging Authority: The Historical Study of Contentious Politics*, pp. 136–148.

Wasserman, S., & Faust, K. 1997. *Social Network analysis: Methods and Applications*, Cambridge University Press.

Weber, K. 2005. A toolkit for analyzing corporate cultural toolkits. *Poetics*, 33(3), pp. 227–252.

Weber, K., & Dacin, M. T. 2011. The cultural construction of organizational life: Introduction to the special issue. *Organization Science*, 22(2), pp. 287–298.

Weber, K., Heinze, K. L., & DeSoucey, M. 2008. Forage for thought: Mobilizing codes in the movement for grass-fed meat and dairy products. *Administrative Science Quarterly*, 53(3), pp. 529–567.

Weber, M. 1978. *Economy and Society: An Outline of Interpretive Sociology*. University of California Press.

Weick, K. E. 1995. *Sensemaking in Organizations*. Thousand Oaks, CA: Sage Publications.

Weick, K. E., & Browning, L. D. 1986. Argument and narration in organizational communication. *Journal of Management*, 12(2), pp. 243–259.

Westphal, J., & Park, S. H. forthcoming. *Symbolic Management: Governance, Strategy, and Institutions*. Oxford, UK: Oxford University Press.

Whetten, D. A. 2000. *Developing Management Skills for Europe*. 2nd ed. Financial Times/ Prentice Hall.

Whetten, D. A., & Godfrey, P. C. 1998. *Identity in Organizations: Building Theory through Conversations*. Sage.

White, H. C. 1992. *Identity and Control: A Structural Theory of Social Action*. Princeton, NJ: Princeton University Press.

Wooten, M., & Hoffman, A. J. 2008. In R. Greenwood, C. Oliver, K. Sahlin, & R. Suddaby, eds., *The SAGE Handbook of Organizational Institutionalism*. London, England: SAGE, pp. 130–147.

Wry, T., et al. 2010. Institutional sources of technological knowledge: a community perspective on nanotechnology emergence. In *Technology and Organization: Essays in Honour of Joan Woodward*. Emerald Group Publishing Limited, pp. 149–176.

Wry, T., & Lounsbury, M. 2013. Contextualizing the categorical imperative: Category linkages, technology focus, and resource acquisition in nanotechnology entrepreneurship. *Journal of Business Venturing*, 28(1), pp. 117–133.

Wry, T., Lounsbury, M., & Glynn, M. A. 2011. Legitimating nascent collective identities: Coordinating cultural entrepreneurship. *Organization Science*, 22(2), pp. 449–463.

Wry, T., Lounsbury, M., & Greenwood, R. 2011. The cultural context of status: Generating important knowledge in nanotechnology. *Status in Management and Organizations*, pp. 155–190.

Wry, T., Lounsbury, M., & Jennings, P. D. 2014. Hybrid vigor: Securing venture capital by spanning categories in nanotechnology. *Academy of Management Journal*, 57(5), pp. 1309–1333.

Yoon, B., & Park, Y. 2005. A systematic approach for identifying technology opportunities: Keyword-based morphology analysis. *Technological Forecasting and Social Change*, 72(2), pp. 145–160.

Zald, M. N., & Lounsbury, M. 2010. The wizards of Oz: Towards an institutional approach to elites, expertise and command posts. *Organization Studies*, 31(7), pp. 963–996.

Zhao, E., Fisher, G., Lounsbury, M., & Miller, D. 2017. Optimal distinctiveness: Broadening the interface between institutional theory and strategic management. *Strategic Management Journal*, no. 38: 93–113.

Zhao, E. Y., Ishihara, M., & Lounsbury, M. 2013. Overcoming the illegitimacy discount: Cultural entrepreneurship in the US feature film industry. *Organization Studies*, 34(12), 1747–1776.

Zhou, M. 2004. Revisiting ethnic entrepreneurship: Convergencies, controversies, and conceptual advancements 1. International Migration Review, 38(3), pp. 1040–1074. Available at: http://dx.doi.org/10.1111/j.1747-7379.2004.tb00228.x.

Zietsma, C., & Toubiana, M. 2018. The constitutive, the energetic and the valuable: Exploring the impact and importance of studying emotions and institutions. *Organization Studies*, 39, 427–443.

Zietsma, C., et al. 2017. Field or fields? Building the scaffolding for cumulation of research on institutional fields. *Academy of Management Annals* 11(1), 391–450.

Zilber, T. B. 2007. Stories and the discursive dynamics of institutional entrepreneurship: The case of Israeli high-tech after the bubble. *Organization Studies*, 28(7), pp. 1035–1054.

Zimmerman, M. A., & Zeitz, G. J. 2002. Beyond survival: Achieving new venture growth by building legitimacy. *Academy of Management Review*, 27(3), pp. 414–431.

Zott, C., & Huy, Q. N. 2007. How entrepreneurs use symbolic management to acquire resources. *Administrative Science Quarterly*, 52(1), pp. 70–105. Available at: www.jstor.org/stable/20109903.

Zucker, L. G., & Darby, M. R. 2007. *Nanobank Data Description, Release 1.0 (Betatest)*. UCLA Center for International Science, Technology, and Cultural Policy and Nanobank.

Zucker, L. G., & Darby, M. R., Furner, J., Liu, R. C., & Ma, H. 2007. Minerva unbound: Knowledge stocks, knowledge flows and new knowledge production. *Research Policy*, 36(6), pp. 850–863.

Zuckerman, E. W. 2016. Optimal distinctiveness revisited: An integrative framework for understanding the balance between differentiation and conformity in individual and organizational identities. In M. G. Pratt et al., eds. *Oxford Handbook on Organizational Identity*, pp. 283–299.

1999. The categorical imperative: Securities analysts and the illegitimacy discount. *American Journal of Sociology*, 104(5), pp. 1398–1438.

2017. The categorical imperative revisited: Implications of categorization as a theoretical tool. In *From Categories to Categorization: Studies in Sociology, Organizations and Strategy at the Crossroads*. Emerald Publishing Limited, pp. 31–68.

Acknowledgments

We would like to thank many scholars who have helped us refine our arguments. First, we would like to thank Royston Greenwood and Nelson Phillips for inviting us to consider more fully fleshing out our ideas on cultural entrepreneurship that have contributed to a now sizeable literature at the interface of organization theory and entrepreneurship. Their guidance has been extremely helpful. In addition, we would like to express our appreciation to Howard Aldrich, Raghu Garud, Thomas Gegenhuber, Joel Gehman, Vern Glaser, Derek Harmon, Benson Honig, Ania Husak, Dev Jennings, Jason Owen-Smith, Mark Mizruchi, Henri Schildt, Patricia Thornton, Eero Vaara, and Jim Westphal who provided many useful insights about how to better structure and expand the scope of our arguments. We have done our best to incorporate their comments and suggestions, and hope we have done enough to seed the development of even more scholarly tributaries in the study of entrepreneurial processes and possibilities.

Cambridge Elements ≡

Organization Theory

Nelson Phillips
Imperial College London

Nelson Phillips is the Abu Dhabi Chamber Professor of Strategy and Innovation at Imperial College London. His research interests include organization theory, technology strategy, innovation, and entrepreneurship, often studied from an institutional theory perspective.

Royston Greenwood
University of Alberta

Royston Greenwood is the Telus Professor of Strategic Management at the University of Alberta, a Visiting Professor at the University of Cambridge, and a Visiting Professor at the University of Edinburgh. His research interests include organizational change and professional misconduct.

Advisory Board
Paul Adler, USC
Mats Alvesson, Lund University
Steve Barley, University of Santa Barbara
Jean Bartunek, Boston College
Paul Hirsch, Northwestern University
Ann Langley, HEC Montreal
Renate Meyer, WU Vienna
Danny Miller, HEC Montreal
Mike Tushman, Harvard University
Andrew Van de Ven, University of Minnesota

About the Series
Organization theory covers many different approaches to understanding organizations. Its focus is on what constitutes the how and why of organizations and organizing, bringing understanding of organizations in a holistic way. The purpose of *Elements in Organization Theory* is to systematize and contribute to our understanding of organizations.

Cambridge Elements $\equiv$

Organization Theory

Elements in the Series

A full series listing is available at: www.cambridge.org/EORT

Printed in the United States
By Bookmasters